GREAT MILITARY CLASSICS

Surprise

SURPRISE

By

Captain E.D. Swinton, D.S.O., R.E.

Later

Major General Sir Ernest Swinton,
K.B.E., C.B., D.S.O.

PENTAGON PRESS

Surprise / **General Waldemar Erfurth**

First Published in 2017

ISBN 978-81-932939-2-8

Published by
PENTAGON PRESS
206, Peacock Lane, Shahpur Jat
New Delhi-110049
Phones: 011-64706243, 26491568
Telefax: 011-26490600
email: rajan@pentagonpress.in
website: www.pentagonpress.in

Printed at Avantika Printers Private Limited.

Contents

Author's Introduction

The principle of annihilation is the fundamental law of war. It is intimately connected with the principle of surprise.

Surprise is a particularly efficient means of defeating the enemy and as old a method as war itself. The history of war shows that through the centuries, almost all decisive victories have been preceded by successful surprises, despite tactical and strategical changes.

The great importance of surprise in war was strongly emphasised by Clausewitz: "Surprise is more or less at the bottom of all military enterprises." However, Clausewitz asserted that surprise can be better applied in tactics than in strategy. According to him, it is rare that surprises are achieved in the field of grand strategy and military politics.

It is obvious that military surprises can be easily accomplished only if small forces and limited spaces are involved and there are merely minor obstacles to be overcome. That is why tactical surprises occur more often than strategical surprises. In every engagement one should try to surprise the enemy by the deployment of one's own forces and by the unexpected use of one's weapons. This rule is generally accepted and it is hardly necessary to illustrate it by examples taken from recent wars.

Surprise is necessarily less frequent in strategic operations, nor can one take advantage of surprise in the general conduct of war. The history of modern wars shows that the chances of strategic surprise are small indeed. The question might therefore be asked whether in a war which is fought by many millions of soldiers strategic surprises are still possible at all.

This is one of the fundamental questions of modern strategy. For annihilation—which is the chief objective of war—cannot he achieved unless the enemy has previously been surprised. German military regulations consider surprise as "a decisive means" for obtaining great successes. If the possibility of surprise is questionable, the possibility of decisive victory must equally be doubtful. Consequently, the question arises whether with modern mass-armies decisive victories in the style of Cannae can still be won.

Count von Schlieffen[1] who taught the German Army the art of waging war with mass-armies believed in the possibility of strategic surprise under modern conditions. The strategy he had in mind did not aim at the destruction of smaller enemy units, but at the annihilation of the total enemy force. War should be decided in one gigantic battle. Schlieffen tried to understand the fundamentals of a battle of annihilation, not in order to enrich his historical knowledge, but in order to outline the character of future battles. "The basic laws of battle," as Schlieffen summarised the results of his historical research "remained unchanged since Hannibal's victory over the Consul Terentius Varro at Cannae. A battle of annihilation can still be fought according to the same plan which Hannibal devised many centuries ago. The enemy front should not be the objective of the main attack. Neither the main concentration of force nor the reserves should be used against the enemy front. Only the smashing of the enemy's flanks is essential. Annihilation is complete if the enemy is also attacked from the rear." Schlieffen did not particularly stress the importance of surprise. In his numerous historical examples he mentioned surprise only casually, although he sometimes emphasised the importance of taking the enemy by surprise.

BATTLE'S DECISIVE FACTOR

Schlieffen was chiefly concerned with the general aspects of the battle of annihilation. He did not discuss problems of a more specific character, because he feared that details would obscure the clarity of his vision. He sought to answer only one question: What is the general form of a battle of annihilation? How must an army be deployed and what form must the attack take, if the enemy is to be annihilated? But Schlieffen by no means disregarded the preponderant role of surprise.

Hannibal won the battle of Cannae because the Roman commander had been surprised by the deployment of the Carthagian army. Numerical superiority was always "the most decisive factor in battle." (Clausewitz). The Roman leader counted on the vast superiority of his forces. In a speech he delivered before the battle, the Roman expressed full confidence in his coming victory. He expected to defeat the numerically weaker Carthagian army in the Roman tradition, by a heavy frontal attack.

Terentius Varro was surprised when Hannibal weakened his centre and dared to encircle his much stronger opponent in spite of the numerical inferiority of his own forces. The previous battles of the Ticinus and the Trebia had been won as the result of victories of the Carthagian cavalry Over the Roman cavalry. In these battles Hannibal also used encirclement tactics. Then he detached for the attack against the enemy's flanks only cavalry and light troops which made it possible for the Romans to break through his pincers and to salvage a large portion of their army.

At Cannae[2], a Carthaginian victory was already assured when Hannibal's cavalry attacked the Roman rear. Yet the new and therefore surprising feature of his battle was the fact that Hannibal deployed his best troops, not at his centre, but on both of his flanks, where during the first phases of the battle he hid them behind his mounted troops. At a favourable moment, these troops attacked the flanks of the Roman legions. It was only this attack against both flanks of the Roman army that made possible the total annihilation of the enemy. Hannbal lacked absolute numerical superiority, but by his unorthodox arrangement he established relative superiority at the decisive point. When the surprised Roman commander finally realize what the intentions of his opponents were, it was already too late to avoid disaster.

The battle of Cannae clearly shows that decisive victory is not the result of a brilliant strategic idea, nor of its effective and skilful execution alone. Victory is also dependent upon the attitude of the enemy commander, who must be caught unawares and ignorant of the true intentions of his opponent until it is no longer possible for him to act on his own initiative. The blow must fall swiftly and unexpectedly a strength must be met by weakness if a battle of annihilation shall materialize. "To obtain a perfect Cannae it is necessary to have a Hannibal on one side, a Terentius Varro on the other. Both of them, each in his own way, contribute together to the great achievement." (Schlieffen). One belligerent must surprise, the other must be surprised. Only and when the two commanders play these respective roles will a battle lead to the annihilation of one army.

FENCERS' SURPRISE TACTICS

In the introduction to "On War," Clausewitz compares war to a gigantic duel. In a duel for life and death, the normal rules of fencing are not observed. Rather, the fencers try to deceive and fatigue each other by feints and to hit suddenly and surprisingly at a vital spot. It is not different in war. Great commanders always distinguish themselves in the art of surprising their enemy. They hide their intentions and measures until the hour of decision comes. Only those commanders act openly who are absolutely certain of victory.

In Clausewitz' opinion, surprise is possible only under favourable conditions. In addition to a good strategic idea and it energetic execution, many conditions are necessary which cannot be influenced or changed by the commander. Luck and merit on one side, mistakes, negligence and ill luck on the other, are the conditions in which surprise may be successful. The effects of surprise are multiplied by the mistakes of the opponent. This is the reason why Schlieffen taught that to achieve victory, it is merely necessary to exploit the enemy's errors. The enemy must be attacked if he has exposed himself by his own mistakes. The attack on unexpectedly exposed weaknesses is a particular form of surprise operation which, however, requires quick action. Otherwise the opportunity may be lost.

The tactical and strategical problems which Schlieffen discussed with his pupils have often been criticised on the ground that he assumed situations which resulted from mistakes committed by both parties. Schlieffen justified himself by pointing out that military history is nothing more than a chain of mistakes and, consequently, every military situation is the product of previous errors. Above all, the soldier must learn to recognize the mistakes of the enemy and to exploit them, though this may sometimes require departure from accepted military rules. The military leader must indeed be able to rid himself from traditional precepts, yet in doing so, he should never forget that heterodoxy has its limits beyond which it is no longer effective, but becomes dangerous.

"Consul Terentius Varro had many pupils at all times," while examples of Hannibal are much less frequent in the history of war. Can the great Carthaginian leader still serve as a model for modern strategists? Can a decisive victory still be won with the means which have so effectively been applied by his military genius? Are the principles which Count Schlieffen developed in his study on the battle of Cannae still valid under present day circumstances? Is successful surprise still the necessary condition of annihilation? Is annihilation the essential objective in the wars of mass armies? Is superior generalship today characterised by executing manoeuvres which the enemy does not expect? And is even the most brilliant strategic idea futile if the enemy prematurely learns of it? These questions shall be answered in this book.

NOTES

1. Schlieffen: Count von Schlieffen (1833-1913) is the master and to a certain extent, the Creator of the German army. Many of the present generals still received part of their military education from him, Or were, at least, educated in his spirit. Schlieffen tried to imbue tie German Staff with one doctrine and one spirit, so that leadership would never break down even if the

communications between the different leaders were severed.

The reactions of all German leaders were to become identical. In order to achieve this goal, Schlieffen frequently played war-games with his officers and undertook trips to prospective battle-fronts where practical field studies were made. Schlieffen is also the father of the German war plan of 1914, although his plan was applied in a modified form. He had foreseen a war on two fronts against France and Russia and advised the use of three-quarters to four-fifths of the German army against France.

Since the German-French frontier was heavily fortified, thus making quick victory improbable, he planned to use the main strength of the German army for an attack through Belgium by which the French were to be enveloped and possibly encircled. Later on he even thought of marching through Holland so that his offensive wing could still further be strengthened; After his retirement new army corps were raised in Germany and at the beginning of World War I used on the left flank of the German army, which thereby acquired enough defensive power to beat back a strong French offensive. It has been argued that these forces should have been employed on the German right wing, for the attack through Belgium and the decisive battles north of Paris. However, it has been shown that the available transport facilities were already overtaxed and would not have permitted a further strengthening of the German right wing. Ludendorff was the author of the modified Schlieffen plan.

Despite all shortcomings, Schlieffen's doctrine must still be considered as one of the best military doctrines which exist, if not the best. It can be summed up as follows: Form a centre of gravity; concentrate there the greatest superiority you can; attack in the direction of the enemy's flanks and rear and try to envelop and encircle the enemy army; above all, manoeuvre incessantly.

Negatively put: Do not disperse and do not attack frontally; be not afraid of weakening parts of your front if you need strong forces for Concentration, do not wait passively, but take and keep the initiative.

2. Cannae: The battle of Cannae (216 B.C.) in which Hannibal inflicted a major defeat upon the Romans has been discovered as a model of battle strategy by the German historian, Hans Delbrueck. Field Marshal Count von Schlieffen the German chief of stall, 1891-1906, framed the German war doctrine according to this model and tried in his war plan against France to imitate Hannibal's example. The most important characteristic of the battle of Cannae, according to the German doctrine, is the attack against both flanks and the rear of the Romans.

   It must, however, be pointed out that the Germans over-simplified the story of Cannae and that the usual description of this battle is partly not correct and partly unproved by the sources. In particular, it is doubtful whether the Romans actually had substantial numerical superiority.

The orthodox figures are: 80,000 Roman infantry plus 6000 Roman cavalry against 40,000 Carthaginians and 10,000 cavalry. These figures have been computed by assuming the size of a Roman legion as ten thousand men. However, more recent studies refute this assumption. The most probable figures are: 40,000 to 50,000 Romans against 35,000 to 40,000 Carthaginians, plus the cavalry as indicated above. This makes the Roman superiority much less impressive, and particularly so because Hannibal was superior in cavalry, the decisive weapon.

To the Roman defeat many more factors contributed than the attack on the flanks. First of all, the two Roman commanders were on bad terms, each of them pursuing his own strategy. Terentius Varro was a political general who had been appointed through public pressure and who was being forced to accept battle on account of the home situation.

Hannibal's battle plan on the other hand, was successful because the disposition of his troops was skilfully concealed from the enemy. However, had the Roman infantry which broke the Carthaginian centre not been seized by panic, Hannibal would hardly have won his battle.

Panic, therefore, is certainly as important a factor as the attack on the flanks. So far as the attack on the Roman rear is concerned, it must be emphasised that according to some sources Hannibal actually used a ruse for getting behind the Roman lines. Just before the battle began, parts of his cavalry pretended to desert to the Romans who had no time in which to investigate thoroughly. They placed the "deserters" behind the battlefield. When the battle was approaching its climax, the deserters" drew short swords which they had hidden and charged the Romans from the rear.

At any rate, there is little doubt that the victory of Cannae was due to rather exceptional circumstances. The Germans themselves acknowledge that in the time between 216 B.C. and 1914 A.D. only the battle of Sedan in 1870 can be compared to it. Consequently, many victories were won according to quite different patterns. And it must be added that Cannae did not decide the war, though this battle figures in history as a "decisive" victory.

Hannibal could not brat the Romans. Fourteen years later he was himself beaten by Scipio. This is to show that foreign readers of German military literature should nut accept the German tradition of Cannae without qualification. Cannae may well be the pattern of an ideal battle; it is certainly not the pattern of battle as such, nor is it the only way to victory.

I

Surprise as Means for Victory in Recent Wars

Surprise, in Clausewitz' opinion, is a product of secrecy and speed. It is of extreme importance to hide one's own plans from the enemy until he is unable to take effective counter-measures. This can be done either by concealment and camouflage or by deception. The enemy is easily deceived if be does not expect a particular decision. Yet if the existence of a decision is in the air, if everybody talks and knows about it, the enemy is seldom deluded. If a military decision is executed with the utmost speed, the chances are that the enemy will be surprised. Secrecy and speed are mutually dependent upon each other. If secrecy cannot be maintained, speed must be increased; if speed is not practical, the enemy must be kept wholly ignorant of the impending operations. Otherwise surprise can never be achieved.

In modern times, secrecy can be maintained only with great difficulties. Too many persons know of the decisions which have been made, even the most secret, inasmuch as the High Command is organised according to the principle of division of labour.[1] As a remedy, every military plan should be executed with extreme speed. Unfortunately at present ideas can not be followed by action as quickly as in earlier wars. The movements of mass armies and the re-grouping of large forces require much time. A great time-lag between the conception of a plan and its execution is unavoidable. This time-lag evidently must affect secrecy. For it will often provide an opportunity for the enemy to discover and frustrate our plans.

Strategic surprise, therefore, in the 20th century became the most difficult military undertaking. The often-discussed mediocrity of generalship in modern wars is to a large degree due to this time-lag between decision and execution which makes strategic surprise next to impossible. In the wars of the 19th century and, of course, in previous wars, strategic surprises were rather frequently accomplished, because wars were then fought in small spaces and during short periods of time. Surprise is obviously much easier under such conditions. But when military preparations must be undertaken in vast areas and over many months, if not years, the maintenance of a military secret must be regarded as an extraordinary achievement.

TIME-LAG GROWS GREATER

The time-lag seems to have much increased during and after World War I. In the last decade, it became more and more difficult to hit the opponent mortally by surprise. Very few brilliant strategic ideas could effectively be put into operation. The danger arose that mass and materiel dominated the ideas of the general, the military machine became too cumbersome for swift adaptations and flexible plans. In one word, the tools became dominant. In Clausewitz' terms, one could say that ideas were being frustrated by frictions of the machine.

What are the result of surprise? Clausewitz asserts that surprise may create the effect of numerical superiority. Without successful surprise no superiority at the decisive point can be achieved. Superiority of numbers is the most general requisite for victory. Absolute superiority *everywhere* is unattainable; hence it must frequently be replaced by relative superiority *somewhere*. To achieve relative superiority somewhere is the main objective of almost all military movements and the essential purpose of generalship. Since relative superiority will hardly be accomplished if the enemy knows the plan of concentration before the hour of attack, the principle of surprise is of importance equal to that of the principle of concentration. To defeat the enemy, he must be attacked with superior numbers at the decisive point; but to possess superior forces at the point of attack, the enemy must be surprised. Annihilation is not possible without previous surprise.

Surprise, however, is not a means for the offensive only. An army on the defensive fights for victory as well as its opponent and must therefore also try to surprise the enemy. Surprise deployments are a particularly effective method at the disposal of defensive armies.

Surprise is thus an element of equal importance to offensive and defensive warfare. All kinds of surprise can be applied in both forms of war, except the surprise of a sudden and unexpected onslaught at the beginning of war, *Ueberfall* which is an important element of offensive warfare exclusively.

The intellectual consequences of surprise, are sometimes as important as the surprise concentration, or application, of force itself. "When surprise is highly successful," says Clausewitz, "it leads to confusion and breaks the enemy's courage." Usually the intellectual and material results of surprise supplement each other. Together, they are capable of completely reversing a given military situation.

CONFLICTING ORDERS

Frequently, surprise reduces the unity of the enemy forces and induces the commanders of the enemy army to issue conflicting orders. Under modern conditions, this danger is particularly great because the direct influence of the High Command on the battlefield is comparatively weak, modern dispersion-tactics giving subordinate leaders a rather large measure of independence. The general can, but seldom is, personally able to, restore the morale of his troops if their will to fight is paralysed. Modern wars offer many examples of panic which led to the frantic flight of whole armies. One is reminder of Schiller's Talbot, the commander of the English forces, no exclaimed at the sight of his routed and fleeing army:

"They will not hear me—not a man will stand;
Clean-loosed are all the bands of discipline.
As if Hells self had vomited around
Its legions of the damned, delirium wild
Blends in a desperate and senseless rout
The coward and the brave alike. In vain
I strive to muster e'en a tiny band
To rally round me and confront the flood
Of foes who waxing surge into the camp."

(*Maid of Orleans*, Act II, scene 5)

General Archduke Joseph Ferdinand might have spoken similar words when large parts of his panic-stricken 4th Army were thrown back behind the river Styr by the Russians under Brussilov. The Italian General Capello had a like experience in the autumn of 1917 when at the Isonzo his army was seized by panic and could not be halted in its retreat.[2]

Clausewitz was quite right when lie asserted that a commander who possesses moral superiority over his opponent is particularly apt to discourage and outwit the enemy and often even wins when, according to the rules of military art, he should lose. Military disasters are usually preceded by moral collapse on the part of the leaders.

To quote one of Clausewitz' *dicta* which is characteristic of his military ideas: "Only he can surprise who imposes his law on the enemy." "To impose one's own law on the enemy" for Clausewitz is not, identical with having the "initiative" in military operations. The offensive party usually possesses the initiative, but offensive operations are not necessarily advantageous. In Clausewitz' opinion, they are only portable if there is some chance that the enemy might be surprised by the offensive moves. If this is not possible, it is preferable to make decisions later than the enemy and to take the enemy's previous decisions into proper account.

The general who can execute his decisions imposes the law on the enemy. If the enemy is able to carry out his own decisions, the opposing army loses its freedom of action. But which side can execute its plans? That side which makes the least mistakes. A military decision which is poorly performed will miscarry. Faulty dispositions will enable the enemy to take effective counter-measures and may thus lead to reverses. If both sides try to surprise each other, the army that commits the fewest errors will be successful.

NOTES

1. A strategic decision can be taken by a few individuals. Yet many more persons arc necessary to draw up detailed battle orders, and numerous are those who are in charge of preparations and who therefore must gain knowledge of the plan, whether directly or indirectly, by deduction. It has been asserted that approximately 2000 persons knew in advance of the Anglo-American operation against North Africa. This, obviously, is the number of persons who had been officially informed of the enterprise. The number of those who deduced the Allied intentions from many not uncertain indications was probably higher. Thus secrecy can not be obtained by merely "saying nothing". Secrecy requires the systematic confusion and deception of the enemy.

   Secrecy is one of the main conditions of success in war. Yet it is also true that nothing is more abused than the principle of secrecy which frequently serves as a shelter for incompetence. Very often, secretiveness is fantastically exaggerated and without deceiving the enemy, serves only to impair the efficiency of one's army. Sometimes, information about the enemy is withheld from their own officers. Many persons think that a secret or confidential document is for their own use only. "Secrecy" is also an effective instrument for interdepartmental competition. It is therefore in order to quote Lord Fisher's remarks on "secrecy and secretiveness":

   "There are three types of secrecy: I, The Ostrich; II, The Red Box; III, The Real Thing.

   "I. The ostrich buries his head in the sand of the desert when pursued by his enemy, and because he can't see the enemy concludes the enemy can't see him! Such is the secrecy of the secretive and detestable habit which hides from our own officers what is known to the world in other navies.

   "II. The secrecy of the Red Box is that of a distinguished Admiral who, with great pomp, used to have his red despatch box carried before him (like the umbrella of no African King), as complaining time most secret plans; but one day, the box being unfortunately capsized and burst open, the only contents that fell out were copies of "La Vie Parisienne! Such, it is feared, was the secrecy of those wonderful detailed plans for war we hear of in the past as having been secreted in secret drawers, to be brought out when the time comes, and when no one has any time to study them, supposing, that is, they ever existed; and, remember, it is detailed attention to minutiae and the consideration of trifles which spells success.

"III. There is the legitimate secrecy and secretiveness of hiding from your dearest friend the moment and the nature of your rush at the enemy, and which of all the variety of operations you have previously practised with the fleet you wilt bring into play! But all your captains will instantly know your mind and intentions, for you will hoist the signal or spark the wireless message, Plan A, or Plan B, or Plan Z!"

2. The "intellectual consequences of surprise" which General von Erfurth mentions may more accurately be described as "panic". Panics occur very frequently in war and play an important role in almost any battle in which a numerically not inferior army is decisively beaten. In spite of the frequency and importance of panics, few military writers and even fewer official military publications mention or discuss panics which apparently are considered as something shameful and unmilitary. Panics happen with unseasoned and under-armed soldiers and in case troops have not been prepared for the fighting methods of the enemy. They also happen with experienced armies, particularly when the troops are tired and hungry. Generally speaking, panics arc the result of bad leadership and of Jack of confidence on the part of the troops. Good leaders may he transformed into bad leaders, if a successful surprise has overthrown their calculations and sapped their self-confidence.

II

Strategic Surprises, Early Phases of War

At the beginning of a War the enemy can be surprised either with respect to time or to space. The enemy should be ignorant of the date of the zero hour as well as of when hostilities will start or what the deployment of the attacking forces will be. Surprise can also be accomplished by new implements of war and by new fighting-methods. Any one of these surprises may if successful, put the enemy in a difficult position.

Almost all great commanders attempted to surprise their enemies by and at the very outbreak of war. Frederick the Great began every one of the Silesian wars with a surprise attack. Napoleon always tried to take the lead over his enemies by sudden onslaughts. Moltke won his decisive victories in the early phases of his wars—a fact which is the basis of the erroneous belief on the part of many pre-World War I writers that quick decisions can still be won as in the period of mass-armies.

After the naval surprise with which Japan in 1904 began the war against Russia, the question whether war should be begun with or without a formal declaration of war was being widely discussed. The Japanese attack without the formality of first declaring war was, however, not a historic novelty. In former times, diplomatic niceties in this connection were rarely observed, and even in the so-called "progressive" centuries many governments failed to deliver a solemn declaration of war. When in 1801 England intended to break the alliance with the Scandinavian countries, the British navy first took up battle positions, and only then, in order to save appearances, was an ultimatum delivered to the Danish government. This ultimatum contained terms which the Danes could not be expected to accept. After, as foreseen, the Danes rejected the British ultimatum, Nelson began immediately to attack the Danish fleet and bombed the fortifications of Copenhagen. (April 2, 1801). This action is a good example of a naval surprise-offensive in peacetime.

WAR IN PEACE-TIME

Some years later, Denmark was again the object of precipitate military violence in time of peace. In order to increase the effectiveness of the *guerre de course* against Napoleon I, the British government on July 19, 1807, decided to ask the surrender of the Danish fleet. The Ships were to remain in British custody for the duration of the war against Napoleon. After this decision was taken, the royal navy anchored in the harbour of Helsingor. Transports carrying 20,000 soldiers followed the navy. The British envoy presented terms to the Danish government and warned that, should the ultimatum be rejected, violence would again be used. The Danish government again refused to submit. Thereupon the British expeditionary forces were landed. On August 24, 1807, Copenhagen was encircled, in the evening of September 2, (that is, technically speaking, still in time of peace) bombardment of the city began. Immense fires were started and many persons were killed. Finally on September 7, an agreement was drawn up according to which the Danish warships and all naval materiel and installations in Danish possession were surrendered to the British. Danish sea power was annihilated for the time being and was never fully restored. Daird Clowes, the greatest British authority on naval history at the beginning of the 20th century, considers the legality of the British attack on Copenhagen as open to discussion, but thinks that this attack was a wise and indeed necessary measure.

The sea battle of Navarino which preceded the Russian-Turkish

War of 1828-29 was also a battle in peacetime. This battle was the outcome of political tension which resembled somewhat the political situation at the time of the Spanish Civil War, 1936-39. Great Britain, France and Russia had signed a pact to protect Greece from Turkish oppression. Thereupon the Turkish-Egyptian navy, accompanied by an Egyptian landing force under command of Ibrahim Pasha, entered the tort of Navarino at the western coast of Morea. Admiral Codrington, commander of the British naval forces in the Mediterranean, informed the Turkish Pasha that the Allies would not permit the Turkish-Egyptian navy to support Turkish land operations against the Greeks. During several weeks the British and French squadrons stood guard over Ibrahim Pasha's navy. On October 14, 1827, a Russian squadron joined the Allies and the Bay of Navarino was effectively blockaded. However, the prospect of maintaining a winter blockade did not particularly please the Allied admirals. They decided to force Ibrahim Pasha to give in. On October 17, 1827, they sent him an ultimatum of sorts. Unfortunately, their communication did not reach the Pasha who was ashore and thus unable to reply promptly. Disregarding this particular circumstance, the Allied warships sailed into the bay. The Turks notified the Allies that the entry of the whole Allied fleet into the bay would not be permitted, although some of the Allied ships might enter if they liked. The British admiral curtly replied that he came to give, not receive, orders. Should a single shot be fired against Allied warships, he added, the Turkish fleet would be destroyed. The Allied ships continued to move in closer to the Turkish navy. Codrington's flagship "Asia" set anchor alongside the Turkish flagship. Again, the vice commander of the Turkish navy officially demanded what were the intentions of the Allies. Suddenly shots were fired and a general engagement began. The Turks fought as well as they could. Finally they succumbed to the superiority of the Allies.

The net result of this surprise attack was the destruction of the Turkish fleet which, without previous declaration of war, was sent to the bottom. The British admiral who was responsible for this deed was decorated by the Allied governments. Yet he was severely reprimanded by British public opinion and eventually he was recalled. After all, the destruction of the Turkish fleet served better the interests of Russia than of England. The liberty of movement which the Russians enjoyed in the Black Sea during the Russian-Turkish War was granted to them by the British admiral.

OFFICIAL WAR DECLARATIONS

After the battle of Navarino none of the Allied Powers delivered an official declaration of war; nor did Turkey. It was only half a year later, on April 26, 1828, that Russia formally declared war on Turkey.

The Japanese attack on the Russian navy at Port Arthur, of all the powers, particularly offended Great Britain. Article 1 of the Third Agreement of the Second Hague Convention, signed on October 18, 1907, was largely due to British influence. It provided that "the contracting Powers recognize that hostilities between them must not commence without previous and explicit warning, in the form either of a reasoned declaration of war or of an ultimatum with conditional declaration of war."

This agreement is probably the reason why, at the outbreak of World War I, declarations of war were delivered in volume for which there is hardly a historical precedent. Any delivery of a declaration of war obviously has definite disadvantages. The power which delivers the first declaration of war is often held responsible for the war itself, although it hardly needs elaboration to show that war guilt not necessarily must have relationship to the first declaration of war. Outsiders and the general public prefer to overlook the true causes of war, particularly in a period of political tension. The factors which really are at the bottom of war are revealed only when secret archives have been opened to historical research. Wise and far seeing governments will therefore avoid taking upon themselves the blame of delivering the first declaration of war. Public indignation can be so easily aroused that it is not advisable to take such a risk.

PRE-WAR DIPLOMACY

The prudence with which, for instance, Bismarck always dealt with this difficult problem is instructive. In 1870, by artful manoeuvres he forced the French government to declare war on Prussia, though he himself considered this war as unavoidable. In 1866, he was particularly careful to prevent Prussia from being considered the aggressor, thus taking into account the political situation in Europe and Germany as well as the wish of his king who desired that "the honour of firing the first cannon shot should be left to the Viennese court." Bismarck treated each of his prospective opponents with special and appropriate methods and succeeded in outwitting every one of them.

Even though by May, 1866, the armies of Austria and her Allies feverishly were preparing for war against Prussia, Bismarck did not yet resort to military counter-measures. He preferred to continue diplomatic conversations, which he could exploit for putting the responsibility for the war on the shoulders of his opponents. Despite the fact that Austria's military preparations were far in advance, Prussia mobilised her forces only step by step, always taking a new provocation on the part of Austria as a welcome pretence for proceeding further.

From a military point of view, the Prussian army's position became more and more difficult. The Austrian army was at last entirely ready for attack, together with the armies of other German states which had had enough time for completely mobilizing their forces and which could, in Moltke words, "measure up to realities." Prussia was thus menaced by war on many fronts, an unpleasant situation which, from the narrow point of view of the army, would have required immediate action. Bismarck did not accede to the desires of the soldiers. Here Prussia purposely renounced the advantages that may result from a surprise attack. Her soldiers were not permitted to begin active operations before Bismarck was convinced that he had exhausted all diplomatic possibilities and that the war guilt was definitely put on Austria. The Austrian government, in order to counteract Prussian pressure on smaller German states, saw itself obliged formally to declare that Austria would give assistance to all countries at war with Prussia. This statement was interpreted by Bismarck as an Austrian act of aggression. According to him, Austria had proved her "hatefulness by aggression."

In Bismarck's interpretation, the Austrian statement was almost a formal declaration of war. At any rate, it was depicted as a notification that a state of war *did* exist between Prussia and Austria. Hence there was no reason why Prussia should furthermore retard her military operations. Bismarck informed the commanders of the three Prussian armies earmarked for operations against Austria that a state of war had come into existence between the two countries and directed them to act accordingly. He also directed the military authorities to deliver to the Austrian advanced guards a letter for the Austrian commander-in-chief. This letter in which the Austrian statement was quoted closed with the following words: "This declaration [of the Austrian government] officially announces the existence of a state of war between our two countries. The signer of this letter [that is, a Prussian officer] has the honour to notify Your Excellency that the Royal Prussian Army has received orders to act accordingly." This method of beginning war by delivering a *lettre d'adieu* to the enemy commander, historically speaking, was extraordinary and unique. Usually events move much too quickly to permit so slow a procedure.

SERBIA'S HARD PROBLEM

During World War I the advantages of strategic surprise-attacks were considered on several occasions. To the beginning of September, 1915, the Serbian army concentrated its main forces against Austria-Hungary. Bulgaria entered the war on the side of the Central Powers. The Serbian High Command planned to attack Bulgaria before the mobilisation of the Bulgarian army could possibly be completed. The Serbs occupied strong defensive positions covered by the three rivers, Drina, Save and Danube.

The strength of the Serbian positions would have made possible the concentration of large forces against the Bulgarians without exposing the Serbian army to an Austrian attack. Such a manoeuvre was the best possible way to forestall a concentric attack from several directions by superior forces. Serbia's allies, however, Russia in particular, objected, in the vain hope that the Bulgarian government might at the last minute change its mind. In view of the future policy of Greece, it was deemed advisable to let Bulgaria, and not Serbia, play the role of aggressor.

Only the Russian High Command wholeheartedly supported the Serbian plan and denounced these delaying tactics. Not to undertake a promising preventive offensive, and to leave Bulgaria complete freedom of action, appeared to be a serious military blunder. The Russian Foreign Minister, Sasonoff, did not share this opinion and even declared that he would consider a preventive attack on Bulgaria a "crime". The Serbian High Command was thus obliged to defend a line of more than 650 miles by means of passive defensive only. Hence the Serbian army was confronted by an insurmountable task. By a purely passive attitude, the approaching concentric attack of the Central Powers against Serbia could not be thwarted, nor could an effective surprise be staged. Schlieffen warned against static defence when he said: "If the enemy is to be surprised, one must not stay in fixed positions, but unceasingly move and manoeuvre."

After World War I the question whether war should be begun by surprise attacks was widely discussed in military literature. Time and again, French military experts discussed this problem and developed the new theory that future wars should and probably would begin by sudden and unexpected attacks ("*attique brusqué*").

An Italian, Ulisse Guadagnini, has given a particularly radical form to the concept of the surprise war. He developed the interesting idea that war should be planned like an ambush. On principle, the first attack of the war should only be launched when and if the opponent does not expect it, thinking that peace is not menaced by any military design on the part of the neighbour. War should erupt suddenly, as a thunderstorm develops in the mountains or as an earthquake occurs, not preceded by warning signals. The army, the navy, the whole people even, must be able to transform themselves with the shortest delay from potential into actual energy—like an explosive charge.

Moral considerations have validity only in civilian life and should not interfere with preparations for war. There are no international laws to prevent a stronger and more powerful people or a better-equipped army from attacking and defeating an inferior opponent. He who would win should not suffer from moral inhibitions. A sudden and unexpected attack is a decisive factor of victory and it will necessarily apply in any future war.

"Without giving the opponent the slightest cause for apprehension beforehand, the aggressor must strike with all his forces and with extreme violence at a previously determined day and at a pre-arranged hour." The mortal blow must be struck before the enemy even knows that war is on. The enemy's military power must be so severely hit that he will be unable to retaliate. Guadagnini emphasised the necessity of striking by surprise with both land and naval forces. He was more skeptical with respect to the chances of surprise by aviation.

In sharp contrast to Guadagnini, another Italian, Giulia Douhet, firmly believed in the decisive role of air-power. According to him, air battle must precede battles on land and sea. After the airpower of one belligerent has been destroyed, his land and sea forces are at the mercy of the master of the air.[1]

EXPLOITING SURPRISE

Once the decision has been taken to wage war, all air forces must immediately attack the enemy nation and, without bothering about declaring war, exploit the possibilities of surprise to the utmost.

The theory of victory through an unexpected offensive in time of peace has, however, obvious weaknesses.

Under modern conditions, thorough large-scale military preparations can hardly be undertaken without knowledge of the enemy. It will be extremely difficult to accumulate a large amount of "potential energy," as Guadagnini wishes, and keel) this accumulation secret. At present, and probably also in the future, distrust is a very powerful factor in international relations. The neighbor is often suspected of having evil intentions which actually he does not have. Large-scale preparations for big offensive are likely to be discovered almost immediately, and one may be sure that such a discovery will lead to Counter-measures.[2]

On the other hand, moral considerations retain a greater importance than many modern writers are inclined to admit. After all, one can never be sure of victory. Even a statesman who is firmly convinced that his country is going to win will hesitate to disregard entirely moral traditions. A country which launches a surprise attack will internationally be denounced as the aggressor and, in case of defeat, may be held fully responsible and to account for its actions. If the surprise attack is not, wholly successful, severe reprisals will be taken against the country guilty of the breach of peace. The theory that might is identical with right and that the stronger can do with the weaker whatever he likes, has not been universally accepted in the history of mankind. For all these reasons, it is easier to advise that moral standards be disregarded than to accept such counsel. Few statesmen will be willing to embark upon a surprise-attack in the midst of peace.

The doctrine of the ambush-war has assumed many different forms, Some of its partisans concede that a single surprise-blow, however strong, is unlikely fully to defeat a strong enemy. Yet a surprise offensive may make possible the seizure of important regions near the frontier and of objectives of high military value to the opponent. The Austrian, General Alfred Krauss, was of the opinion that in 1914 Austria should have begun the war by the immediate occupation of Belgrade. According to him, the capture of this city would have been the best start for the Austrian army.. "Serbia's capital, with the headquarters of all Serbian authorities and with its important archives was separated from Hungary only by the river Save, that is to say, by approximately 600 yards. The seizure of the Serbian archives would have been of inestimable political value, while the early crossing of the Save and the establishment of a bridgehead in Belgrade would have been of equally inestimable military value.

Another Austrian, General Conrad von Hoetzendorf, on August 10, 1916, proposed to the German Chief of Staff to march into Rumania immediately after the conclusion of an alliance between Rumania and the Entente should officially be confirmed by the Rumanian radio. His plan was to attack with the German forces under Mackensen from northern Bulgaria across the Danube and to advance toward Bucharest. At the same time, Austrian and Hungarian units, reinforced by German detachments, would attack eastward from Transylvania, moving equally to Bucharest. The Austrian was convinced that this operation would catch Rumania napping and lead to important quick successes. The German High Command, at first, did not expect Rumania to enter the war. On August 18, they sent a belated and dilatory reply and practically declined Hoetzendorf's idea. His plan was criticised by the official Austrian publication on the history of the World War, on the ground that it would have required the presence of ready and powerful forces in Transylvania and northern Bulgaria which were not available at that time. Still, it is conceded that an attack of that kind could have been very successful.[3]

MISSION OF FRONTIER TROOPS

Swift action at the outbreak of war is generally considered as an indispensible feature of effective defence. Very early it became customary to station troops near the frontier. In case of enemy attack, these covering units were assigned to the task of disrupting the enemy's mobilisation schedule—and, if possible, pushing his forces back. The experience in 1870 that France had with such an arrangement was far from satisfactory. The hasty advance of

French units not yet fully mobilised caused general confusion. The mobilisation centres and railway stations were crowded with reservists unable to join their units, because they did not know where they could find them. The army corps and divisions lacked the most essential transport services, their field hospitals and administrative personnel. No provisions were made for the feeding of the troops. Maps were not available.

After some days, the Ministry of War in Paris did not know what to do; they left all decisions to the troops and the field-officers themselves, hoping that they would be able to muddle through. However, the confidence in the *"on se débroullier"* was disappointing. The chaos was not disentangled. At last, the French High Command realised that, instead of taking the war quickly across the Rhine into Germany, the French army had to defend French soil in France. The strategic surprise-attack which the French had planned in 1870 thus was frustrated by the frictions of their own military machine.

The German *coup de main* against Liège in 1914 is an example of a successful surprise operation at the beginning of war. The troops selected for this enterprise were assembled during the third day after the proclamation of general mobilisation (August 4), while still in their peace-time formation. In the night of August 5-6, they were ordered to surprise and break through the outworks of the fortress and to seize the town and its transport-facilities. This bold and reckless operation was accomplished despite almost insurmountable difficulties and local setbacks. It could easily have failed. Its success was chiefly due to the energy of one man, Ludendorff, who had conceived the whole plan himself. Besides, it was executed by first-class units and, in some respects, favoured by luck. The *coup de main* against Liège is one of the very few successful examples of its kind. Consequently, it must be considered as an exception, not as a generally applicable precept.[4]

For sometime prior to World War I, the concentration of Russian cavalry divisions near the German eastern frontier often gave cause to apprehensions on the part of the German government. In his time, Bismarck, as Chancellor, felt himself responsible for the military preparedness of the Reich and repeatedly drew the attention of the German War Minister to the possibility that East Prussia might be invaded by Russian cavalry. He prevailed upon the Minister to take necessary precautions against that danger. The German General Staff was, of course, constantly concerned with the same problem. In 1894, Count Schlieffen travelled with the General Staff in eastern Germany in order to study the problems which would arise for Germany's defence in case Russian cavalry had invaded Prussia and accomplished the partial destruction of the railroad system before the German army was mobilised. Schlieffen did not consider a Russian cavalry offensive as likely, or dangerous.. The events of August, 1914, showed how right he was in this assumption. To be sure, Russian cavalry tried to cross the boundary and, by destroying railroad facilities, to disrupt mobilisation and deployment of the German army. But the German frontier-guards were prepared, and the Russian cavalry achieved but poor results One Russian cavalry division was beaten on August 5, near Soldau, another on August 9, near Bialla.

DEFENCE BECOMES STRONGER

In modern military literature surprise raids across the frontier during the first days of war are frequently discussed and sometimes recommended, because, under modern conditions, they can be carried out by mechanised and motorised units. Speed and the fire-power of modern mechanised equipment are, of course, incomparably stronger than those of the old-time cavalry. The power of mechanised weapons is sometimes considered as, a promise that surprise raids, which formerly were seldom effective, can now be successfully performed. One should, however, not forget that the defence against modern offensive weapons also has become much stronger than it was in 1914 and that no country will neglect the protection of its frontiers. Provided both sides are equally cautious and either side is unable to begin its mobilisation substantially in advance, modern mechanised units are not likely to be more successful than the Russian cavalry in 1914.

The early beginning of the Russian offensive in August, 1914, was largely due to French pressure. The French needed a strong diversion on the eastern front in order to resist the German attack in the west. The director of the Russian Bureau of Military Operations, General Dobrorolski, reported that the Russian army was not prepared to take the field before August 28. The French, however, insisted on accelerating the Russian operations. General Shilinsky, a former chief of the Russian General Staff, who had negotiated the military alliance with France and who in August, 1914, was the commander of the Russian armies operating against East Prussia advanced the date of his Offensive to August 17.

The Russian First Army began to move; the Second Army crossed the frontier on August 18 and 19. The results of this precipitated action were far from satisfactory. As a consequence of their forced marches, the Russian troops, in particular those of the Second Army, were tired and insufficiently supplied. Nevertheless, the Second Army continued its marches across the difficult and almost roadless regions near the German frontier. The Russian troops suffered from the immense heat of August. On August 21, the Chief of Staff of the Second Army, General Posdovsky, was forced to declare that, due to the exhaustion of the troops, the continuation of the advance would be an adventure". General Samsonoff, commander of the Second Army, shared this opinion and asked the. High Command for one day's rest. This request was rejected. Consequently, the Russian Second Army entered the battle of Tannenberg in a state of exhaustion and with insufficient supplies. Under the circumstances, catastrophe was hardly avoidable.

A postponement of the Russian offensive by four days would not have been a disadvantage for the Russians. Our present knowledge about the battle of Tannenberg certainly justifies this conclusion.

The history of modern war offers not a single example of a

successfully precipitated offensive undertaken with units either not yet fully mobilised or mobilised more quickly than the rest of the army. There are many examples to the contrary. In the most favourable cases, precipitated offensive action led to momentary and local advantages, but only at the cost of disturbing one's own mobilisation and deployment.

Precipitation will hardly yield better results in future wars. Success in war usually goes to the side which uses its power in a premeditated and coordinated way.

SURPRISES BY SEA

The obstacles which prevent quick and early land operations are insignificant in comparison with the obstacles to surprise-attacks over sea. In an illuminating article, entitled "Naval Surprise Attacks at the Beginning of War," General von Janson discussed Japan's naval surprise attack against Russia in 1904. The success of this operation, which actually started the war, was due to exceptional conditions. It is unlikely that similar conditions will ever exist again before a war between the great western powers. Besides, the distant coastal areas of Asiatic Russia are hard to defend from European Russia where the sources of Russia's military power are situated. The geographical conditions of the Russian empire permitted the Japanese to dispense with a general mobilisation of all their forces. Instead, they mobilised their divisions successively and even dispatched them successively to the front. To be sure, their landing forces in neutral Korea on the Asiatic mainland did not have to fight, but only to secure bases for later operations. A landing on the shores of a western country would immediately be followed by a difficult battle with a strong military force. The Russians were unable quickly to counter-attack the Japanese in Korea, but under normal conditions, the defender will not be slow in concentrating a strong force against the invader.

The mobilisation of large landing forces can remain as little a secret as the assembly of a big convoy of transport ships. Only a direct attack against the enemy navy itself can be carried out with surprise. Before extensive landing operations can be undertaken the enemy fleet must be paralysed if not annihilated.

But such an ambitious goal cannot be reached unless the attacker is assisted by criminal negligence on the part of the defender. And yet, notwithstanding the extraordinary negligence of the Russians, the Japanese did not succeed in completely crippling the Russian navy in Port Arthur. General von Janson proved the hopelessness of a naval surprise-attack under normal western conditions by the indecisiveness of Japans surprise in 1904. The events of World War I did not refute General Janson's thesis of the impracticability of naval surprise attacks. In the meantime, the appearance of military aviation which enables an effective control of all main sea-approaches has facilitated the defence of coastal lines. Naval and air-attacks, even if launched only to gain temporary mastery of the sea and air require extensive preparations. Too, these preparations take such time that their premature discovery can hardly be avoided. Large scale surprise-landings must practically be considered as an impossibility. They are not an appropriate method to win a war during and by its very start.[5]

Aviation offers, however, a better chance for surprise than land and naval weapons. Douhet, the advocate of a surprise offensive with large fleets of aircraft, has still many partisans. Indeed, an air-force is able swiftly to attack unsuspecting opponents, although during a political crisis no country will neglect to perfect extensive air-raid precautions.

Many plausible objections have been raised against an air strategy in Douhet's style. The danger of reprisals, for instance, should not be overlooked. On the whole, it is not altogether probable that future wars will be started in accordance with Douhet's recommendations.

ABYSSINIA ITALY AND ENGLAND

The question must also be asked whether future wars, like World War I, will be preceded by the usual diplomatic formalities, from the recall of Ambassadors to the official declaration of war. Every government will leave it to its opponents formally to declare war while the latter will, of course, try not to fall into the trap. The relations between Great Britain and Italy during the Abyssinian War showed that one may even resort to open economic warfare without either side recognizing the existence of a state of war. The history of Far Eastern wars also indicates that a state of war may actually exist, screened as frontier incidents, although no state of war is recognised by the belligerents or the neutrals.

These examples seem to demonstrate that initial surprise attacks arc of questionable military value and can be successful only under rare and exceptional circumstances.

The question then arises whether the enemy can be surprised by a particular and unexpected disposition of the military forces. Schlieffen remarked that the disposition of an army is largely dependent upon the peace-time location of troops, the railroad system and the shape of the frontiers of the attacked country. "If these three factors are known, the offensive deployment of any army can be calculated in its general outlines."

Field Marshal Count von Moltke in 1870 indicated the exact disposition and concentration of the French army. "In order to learn the French war plan," commented Schlieffen, "Moltke paid neither many spies nor did he bribe high officials. To get knowledge of the most important French state secret, he limited his expenses to the price of a cheap railway-map. In the area of railroads the deployment of every army is conditioned by, and dependent upon, the existing railroads."[6]

Before the First World War, the German General Staff deduced the deployment of the French and Russian armies in the same way and later events proved their deductions to have been largely correct. Similar deductions are obviously more difficult with respect to a country lighting on several separate fronts because, comparatively speaking, it is free to decide by its own will against which opponent it shall first concentrate the bulk of its forces.

Consequently, Germany's enemies in 1914 were at a loss correctly to foresee the German war plan. The Russians assumed that the main German forces would be tied up in the west. The Russian General Staff therefore, intended to throw its main forces against Austria-Hungary while Germany was to be attacked only by limited forces. Yet the Russians were not sure of their own deductions and prepared a second substitute war plan in case the Germans should carry their main effort to the east. Then the mass of the Russian army would take the offensive against eastern Prussia.

EFFECTIVE SECRET SERVICE

In order to gain the necessary information in time, the Russians had placed secret agents in all German cities with big garrisons, particularly in Stettin, Posen, Breslau. The agents had to ascertain in what directions the German corps were moved. On August 6, that is to say just four days after general mobilisation had been proclaimed, the Russians already knew that Germany would leave only small forces in the East. The original Russian war plan could therefore be put into operation.

Nor did the French General Staff dare rely on its own guess. To be sure, most French officers were convinced of a German attack through Belgium. However, opinions were divided with respect to the numbers which Germany could spare for the Belgian operation, to the direction of their advance (in particular whether they would operate only on the eastern or on both banks of the Meuse) and to the German attitude in Lorraine. The French therefore devised a plan with two variations. The second variation was to be applied in case of a German attack through Belgium. In addition, they put a whole army in second line for use where needed. The second variation of the French plan was set in motion by August 2, when the Germans asked the Belgian government for free passage through Belgium. Though the uncertainty of the French General Staff was thus dispelled, they continued to ignore, the true German intentions. The French persisted in their belief that large German forces would be concentrated in Lorraine and that the German right flank would not extend beyond the Meuse. "The advance of our strong right flank on the left bank of the Meuse," writes General von Kuhl, "completely surprised the enemy and disrupted his plan of operations."

Surprise through unexpected disposition and concentration of forces is certainly a difficult undertaking, yet it is possible and can be very effective. An army battling on several fronts has the advantages of the inner lines and can, within limits, freely choose the direction of its main effort. The disposition and concentration of armies lighting on the outer lines can, however, be deduced with some probability although, of course, such deductions may be wrong. It follows that surprises can also be performed by an army operating on the outer lines.

The tendency to begin war with surprise attacks was a standard feature of many former wars and still exists in the present period, even though initial surprise-attacks become more difficult. An unorthodox and unexpected disposition of the army puts a means of surprise at the disposal of the commander. On principle, the army should be deployed with a view to surprising the enemy, even if the chances are small that the attempted surprise will succeed.

NOTES

1. Douhet: The Italian, General Giulio Douhet, (1869-1930), is usually considered as the prophet of air power. He indeed as one of the first professional soldiers who recognised the vast military potentialities of aviation. However, his contributions to the emergence of air power were not considerable, except in the field of propaganda. His forecast of future wars and future types of military aircraft were not borne out by facts. He was an enthusiast of his weapon, who had lost almost all sense of proportion, asserting, for instance, that land offensives could be no longer decisive. Yet he was indubitably also a man of vision.
2. Guadagnini: It is obvious that the chances of such a war are much better than General Erfurth assumed. It may be true that preparations for attack are detected before the attack is launched. Yet the defender may not be able to

catch up with the advance of the attacker. A mobilisation with a lead of only a few days may be of inestimable value, at any rate in a war against a country without space. On the other hand, one has seen that for political reasons the defender sometimes does not dare to take counter-measurers and actually may fail to mobilize fully his forces. This happened with Poland. Germany could not be angered with "provocation."

3. Ambush War: Despite General Erfurth's arguments, in the present war Germany as well as her co-belligerants began all their campaigns with a surprise attack, and delivered their official declaration of war only after the operations had already started. And there is no doubt, either, that most of the attacks occurred when they were not yet expected. There is, of course, never a complete surprise. But an advance of a few hours may decisively influence the first battles and enable the attacker to seize immediately important territory.
4. Liege: It is quite true that the *coup de main* on Liège was a hazardous undertaking, for the simple reason that it had not been thoroughly rehearsed and that the troops did not know their tasks. Liege was almost a failure, because the principle of secrecy had been exaggerated. Many of the officers did not know what they were supposed to do and had only insufficient knowledge of the situation. The much more difficult *coup de main* on Eben Emael which the Germans performed in 1940, after thorough rehearsing, shows that similar operations are not chiefly dependent upon luck, but can be successfully accomplished, provided they are carefully planned and studied.
5. Naval Surprises: It is hardly necessary to show that actually the chances for naval surprises are much better. Norway, Pearl Harbour, North Africa would not have been possible, if Erfurth's pessimism were justified.
6. Moltke: Today, Moltke would be hardly as successful with a cheap railway map. There are too many railways and too many highways and military concentrations can be accomplished wherever one likes. Under modern conditions, motorised and mechanised units can partly liberate themselves from railroads and highways. Hence, war plans may now be kept secret easier than they were in Moltke's time.

III

Surprise, War of Movement

Information gathered in peace-time about enemy country is not only incomplete, but loses its value after the enemy army has been deployed and begins to move. With the beginning of hostilities, however, information of the enemy army and country becomes constantly available.

Yet little military information, whether secret or not, can ever be accepted as definite anti reliable. For war takes place in the realm of uncertainty, hence of surprise. "A good deal of the information gathered during war is contradictory; a still greater part of it is erroneous and the bulk of military information is of dubious reliability. Plans which are built upon such ground may fail."

Services of intelligence, whatever their reliability may be, are indispensable in time of war. The more that is known about an opponent, the better are the chances that strategic intentions against him will be effectively carried out and that the enemy will be surprised. Consequently, intelligence and information services should be as effective and efficient as possible. Yet it is one thing to collect abundant detailed information and another to synthesize it into a general picture correctly reflecting the general conditions on the enemy side. The commander-in-chief has the ungrateful task of distinguishing between correct information, wilful lies, exaggerations and errors. From among the numerous and contradictory pieces of information he receives, he is supposed to make a correct selection.[1]

The talent to see things rightly is very rare. Napoleon exclaimed: "*Mais c'est la realité des choses qui commande,*" thus criticizing commanders who base their decisions not upon facts, but upon their own wishful thinking. Most people are more impressed by dramatic events than by sober calculations and cold reasoning. In serious situations they tend to see things as worse than they actually are, while they like to exaggerate their own successes if the developments are more favourable. They lack the quality which Marshal Pilsudsky characterised as a good "*tête froide d'un chef.*" This quality is inborn, but can also be acquired by a long experience in war.

Military situations change rapidly. Very often a commander has taken a decision in view of a given situation. But when he begins to execute his plan, the situation has developed further and he is already confronted by a totally different set of circumstances. Unless he has self-confidence and liberates himself from the impressions of momentary conditions, he will become undecided and hesitate. Clausewitz therefore asked that a true military leader must have confidence in his superior knowledge and be "like a rock that shatters the waves."

OBJECTIVE SELF-CONFIDENCE

Obviously, self-confidence goes hand in hand with the faculty of objectively and soberly appreciating a given situation.

The commander should be able correctly to appraise new information which may modify or change the situation and he must examine it without prejudice to decide whether his original decision is still applicable. It is as wrong to adhere too long to a previously made decision as to relinquish it too early. The history of war shows that self-deception on the part of the High Command is a very definite danger, especially for strong personalities.

Count Schlieffen ironically described the type of military leader who puts trust only in his own intuition and dismisses any information which does not tally with his dreams. "It is wrong to assume," he writes, "that information gained by the cavalry does invariably influence military decisions or is even acceptable. Military leaders often like to depict the situation in a way compatible with their own wishes. If the information they receive strengthens their belief it is joyfully accepted. But if it contradicts their assumptions, it is rejected as entirely wrong and used to prove that the cavalry has again failed in its duties."

Count von Schlieffen wrote these words at a time when cavalry still was the main instrument for reconnaissance. At present, reconnaissance is carried out by other branches of the army. But the experience of former wars which Schlieffen thus described is still valid. The World War I offers many examples of how superior commanders rejected information from their subordinates with the remark that it be only the product of "imagination and pessimism." Warnings were often credited only when it was too late. Commanders suffer frequently from the tendency to be over-optimistic. The consequence usually is that the enemy is able to achieve a surprise, if not against the troops themselves, then against the commanders. A commander who fails to accept warnings, facilitates the winning of a great victory—for the enemy. An erroneous appreciation of the situation is an essential factor of defeat. In recent wars, many successful surprises were made possible by the incredulity of commanding officers.

The difficulty of correctly appraising a military Situation is still one of the main bottlenecks in war. It will continue to remain an essential bottleneck in all future wars.

NOTE

1. Intelligence Service: One of the reasons why high commanders are likely not to accept incoming information must he attributed to the fact that the chief of the intelligence department seldom has equal rank with the commanding officer. In some armies, he is not even a general officer. It also happens that he is Sometimes insufficiently informed of the intentions of the operation department. Care should be taken that close collaboration and incessant consultation between the department of military operation and the intelligence department are assured, and that not as in the French army during World War I, when the Operation Bureau on principle distrusted any information it received from the Intelligence Service. (cf. Pierrefeu).

IV

Deployment for Battle

Up to the time of Moltke, an army usually marched a considerable distance before it reached the battlefield. Since 1914, the open space which formerly separated two fighting armies before they joined in battle has been narrowed down. Railroads have been developed to make possible the deployment of the armed forces in the immediate vicinity of the frontier. The increasing size of armies has made the former assembly in different groups impractical. Continuous fronts are now being established on the very first day of hostilities.

At the beginning of World War I the German and French armies deploying at the Franco-German frontier were separated from each other by a small distance. Therefore deployment in depth was not possible in this area. Further to the north, however, the two armies were separated by the whole width of Belgium.

The right wing of the German army was consequently compelled to march a considerable distance until it could reach the battlefields of the Sambre and Meuse. The corps at the extremity of the German flank between August 12 and August 22 marched approximately one hundred and forty-five miles.

When hostilities began, both sides ignored the condition of the enemy army. Hence both sides, at least in theory, had a good chance of surprising the opponent. Yet none of these many chances was exploited by either side, as we shall see presently.

The German High Command on August 20, learned some

important details of the French plan of concentration. A strong French army was being assembled between Charleroi and Dinant in the triangle between the Sambre and the Meuse. The Belgian army had retired into the fortress of Antwerp. The location of the British Expeditionary Force was not known to the German. High Command. A Belgian newspaper on August 19, had published an official London dispatch on the landing of the British army in France. But the German High Command still ignored the reference to the port of disembarkation as well as the whereabouts of the British units.

The concentration of strong Allied forces at the Franco-Belgian frontier confronted the German right wing with the prospect of a big battle. The German High Command took measures to ensure a well-concerted attack of the three armies forming the right German flank against the enemy forces vest of Namur. The difficulties of this task are not always fully appreciated today because we are influenced by our historical knowledge about the events. In actual battle the situation can never be appraised so easily as is possible later by study of historical books. The exact strength of the opponent, the direction of his movements and his intentions are apt to be unknown during actual operations. Movements in war strongly, resemble a passage through wild, primeval country.

"War is like sailing across an unexplored sea full of reefs which the captain may well divine, but which he has never seen and amongst which he now must navigate in a dark night." (Clausewitz). German leadership had to coordinate the advance of the three armies so that they could effectively be concentrated on the battlefield itself. Field Marshal Count von Moltke considered such a coordinating task as the most difficult undertaking of strategic leadership. Indeed, history shows that a similar task has only seldom been successfully performed.

SHORTENING TIME-LAG

The difficulty lies in the inevitable time-lag between the arrival of one formation at the front and of other formations at the enemy's flank or rear. Count von Schlieffen taught that this time-lag should be shortened by appropriate arrangements on the part of the different army leaders. If the armies approach the battlefield and battle becomes imminent, energetic leadership is necessary to maintain cohesion between the different units. In such a situation the movements of the advancing armies must be coordinated by a strong central command, even if at the cost of interfering with the independence of the army commanders. At least, this was the opinion of Field Marshal Count von Moltke. His own nephew, General von Moltke, however, did not conform to his uncle's precept and assigned the central command of the movements of the German right wing to the senior among the three army commanders, General von Bulow. Since the three German army commanders had different strategic intentions, this solution increased friction on the German side.

Bulow, the commander of the Second Army, did not believe in an early intervention by the British Expeditionary Force. He ordered on August 20, the First and Second Army to move on to the south and then to wait until the Third Army which was still operating in the area of Namur and Givet, could catch up with them. He planned for a later concentric attack against the enemy forces assembled between the Sambre and the Meuse. The First and Second Armies were to attack in a north-southern and the Third Army in an east-western direction. By the evening of August 21, the Second Army had turned around and was facing south. Its advanced guards had crossed the Canal du Centre and the Sambre, where as a consequence of the rashness of subordinate leaders, some fighting had taken place. Bulow on August 22, ordered the First and Second Armies to stop the southward advance and instead to close the gap between the two armies.

All three armies on August 23, were to effect a simultaneous attack on the French south of the Sambre and west of the Meusé. But during the morning of August 22, General von Bulow changed his mind. He had gained the impression that only weak

French forces stood south of the Sambre. He could thus hope to win an important success by launching an immediate attack. Without hesitation, he ordered the resumption of the advance and the capture of the difficult terrain south of the Sambre. The Third Army was directed to attack quickly in the direction of the Meuse. Bulow ignored the fact, however, that the commander of the Third Army could be informed about his new plan only around 12 noon, of August 22. Bulow also counted upon the full cooperation of the First Army.

In the course of August 22 the true disposition of the French Fifth Army became increasingly clear. The Second Army did not meet weak French advanced guards south of the Sambre, but with the mass of the French Fifth Army occupying positions, "worthy of a Terentius Varro." The French positions invited encirclement. The German armies were thus certainly well placed to inflict a crushing defeat on the French Fifth Army. The eastern flank of the French could have been attacked by the Third Army. Had the German First Army advanced quickly, where necessary by forced marches, it could have attacked the western flank of the French positions. Too, had strong available cavalry units been concentrated on the German right flank in order to attack the enemy's rear, all essential conditions for the annihilation of the French Fifth Army would have been created.

DIFFICULTIES OF ENVELOPMENT

In order to achieve a complete Cannae against the French Fifth Army, a frontal attack of the German Second Army, tieing up the main French forces, was indispensable. The frontal attack was the very condition of successful attacks against the French flanks. But the German assaults on the flanks and the rear of the French Fifth Army failed to develop satisfactorily and were too weak to achieve an annihilating victory.

Schlieffen pointed out that to begin envelopment at the right moment and to direct attacking forces in the right direction is the most difficult part in any battle of annihilation. The battle of Mons and Namur proves the accuracy of this view.

Germany lacked a Hannibal who would have been able to coordinate the operations of the three armies. It was wrong to deliver the main attack at the Sambre near Namur and Maubeuge. The main attacks should have been directed against the French flanks. If, to their surprise, the French and British should have been outflanked, a definite success was assured. Yet it was essential that the German flanking marches were carried out during the night of August 22-23. The attack had to be launched on August 23. Had it been retarded longer, the enemy would have avoided the trap. The time-lag between the beginning of the frontal attack and the first attacks on the flanks could under no circumstances be extended beyond that date.

At the end of his study on the Battle of Cannae, Count von Schlieffen summarised the conditions of a successful battle of annihilation. He emphasised that the commander must be assisted by sub-leaders with a strong sense of discipline and a good understanding of his intentions. Only if the situation of the enemy is interpreted similarly by all commanders and if the sub-leaders agree with the commander-in-chief on the plan of operations, is the battle likely to end successfully. Such an agreement was entirely lacking among the German commanders in the battle of Mons and Namur.

General von Kluck held opinions about the enemy situation that differed from those of von Buelow. Von Kluck was convinced that the British Expeditionary Force would soon attack north of Lille. In the hope of avoiding a British attack against his right flank, he stopped his advance on August 21 and left his right wing as a protective force behind his main forces, although, according to Bulow's directions, this wing was to proceed hurriedly to, the south. Indeed, a surprise attack against the Allied left flank could not be accomplished by keeping these forces back.

The opinions of the two commanders were not harmonised during the next days. A stall officer from the High Command tried to adjust the existing differences, but failed to coordinate the strategic ideas of the two generals A coordination would have been possible only by a clear and incontestable order which Bulow, for lack of authority, could not issue. Bulow was merely a *primus inter pares* and could not prevent General von Kluck from making faulty dispositions.

Thus, Kluck maintained his arrangements, although in the meantime it had been ascertained that the British had taken up positions on the western flank of the French Army and could therefore not attack the right wing of Klucks forces. Still, Kluck was not yet convinced and held that the positions of the British left wing were not yet sufficiently known. Consequently, he continued to protect his right flank with considerable :forces which he left far behind his front, instead of dispatching them as quickly as possible to the battlefield. This arrangement was maintained on August 23.[1]

NAPOLEON DEMANDED SPEED

In a similar situation Napoleon had found impressive words to assure absolute obedience to his orders and to make his marshals act with indicated speed. Before the battle of Ligny, Marshal Soult, upon Napoleon's command, sent an urgent appeal to Marshal Ney to direct his immediate advance on to the battlefield: "You must immediately manoeuvre to envelop the flank of the enemy . . . . If you act vigorously, his army is lost. The fate of France is in your hands." On the eve of the battle of Mons a similar order should have been sent to Kluck.

A commander with the necessary *coup d'oeil* was also lacking on the left flank of the German forces. It is a frequent occurrence in the history of war that reality and its recognition through the commander are two entirely different things. The commander of the Third Army did not realize the tremendous possibilities which offered themselves during the battle of Namur. His attention was fully absorbed by the difficulties of his imminent attack across the Meuse near Dinant. To be sure, the Meuse in this region is a very considerable obstacle. The attack had therefore to be methodically prepared. Haste would have been dangerous. Or so it seemed.

August 22 was spent in preparing for the crossing of the Meuse. The attack against the hills dominating the regions west of Dinant was ordered for August 23. Yet, on August 18, it had already been ascertained beyond doubt that the regions south and southeast of Givet were not occupied by the enemy. According to information obtained on August 22, mutually corroborated by cavalry and air reconnaissance, it was confirmed that both banks of the Meuse between Givet and Charleville were free from the enemy.[2]

This valuable information failed to cause the commander of the Third Army to change his plan. However, it should have convinced him that it would be more effective to launch a surprise attack in direction of the gap south of Givet, instead of concentrating the main effort against the strongest part of the enemy front near Dinant. An attack against the open flank of the enemy could have smashed the entire Allied defence position on the Meuse.

GERMANS MINED CHANCES

The dense forests southeast of Givet would have made possible a secret southward advance of strong German formations. Enough time was available to prepare a surprise crossing of the Meuse near Fumay during the night of August 22. This attack would have aimed at the rear of the Fifth French Army. It would have been the most important contribution to a battle of annihilation, ii the style of Cannae. The historical evidence conclusively shows that the French would have been totally surprised by a German attack south of Fumay. And they would have been hit at the most decisive point.

German leadership during August 23 lost the last opportunity to impose its law on the French army.

The previous night the commander of the First Army received

a very important message. He was notified that British troops had occupied positions on the Canal du Centre, that is to say, north and northeast of Mons. Early in the morning a cavalry division reported by radio that the British were in Maubeuge and that the whole territory up to the Scheldt was free from enemy forces.

But even now no decision was taken to accelerate the advance. The commander of the First Army did not think to proceed "*sur-le-champ*" on to the battlefield and without further delay attack the enemy's flank. Instead, he still persisted in waiting for more complete information, in particular about the left wing of the British Army. Complete and detailed information about the enemy is, however, never available in war, unless the enemy himself takes the trouble to furnish it, as the Russians did during the battle of Tannenberg and during the campaign of Lodz by broadcasting it by radio. Normally, "imagination and combination have an important role to play" (Schlieffen).

Before noon on August 23, the commander of the First Army received a report that since August 22, strong enemy forces were being detrained near Tournay. It was not said whether these troops were British or French. This news caused further confusion and hesitation; the advance of the First Army was again stopped. It is opportune here to recall Schlieffen's dictum that "nothing is more dangerous in war than reliable information." For "reliable" information very often turns out to be either wrong or out of date.[3] In point of fact, information did come in which dispelled definitely all doubts about the location of the British forces. After 12 noon the commander of the First Army conclusively knew that the British stood near Mons. He learned in the afternoon that information of the arrival of troops near Tournay had been erroneous. Cavalry reported that no enemy forces were present in the area of Thielt-Kortryk-Tournay. French troops were in the vicinity of Lille.

At last all concern about the security of the First Army was removed. The advance was resumed. Yet the corps in the second line of the First Army were not ordered to push quickly forward, despite the fact that they still lagged far behind. The advance of the right wing of the First Army was also retarded by different counter-orders. Nevertheless, on August 23, the British front near Mons was strongly attacked by the left wing and centre of the German First Army. Yet a decisive victory was impossible without a simultaneous attack by the right wing of the First Army against the enemy flank. This attack could not be launched in time because on the evening of August 23 this wing was still at a distance of twenty to thirty miles from the front.

The German High Command on August 23 twice notified the Third Army of a big gap in the enemy front south of Givet. The High Command advised the Third Army to cross the Meuse south of Givet "in order to cut the retreat of the enemy forces."

On the other hand, the commander of the Second Army pressed General von Hausen, the commander of the Third Army, to advance rapidly in a westerly direction. Obviously, these two requests were somewhat contradictory.

Hausen was thus faced with the alternative of continuing his frontal attack near Dinant towards the west or of following the advice of the High Command, cross the Meuse south of Givet and then attack to the northwest. Hausen first decided to accede to the request of the Second Army and to continue his frontal attack near Dinant. After a second message from the High Command he modified his decision and ordered those parts of his forces which were not tied up at Dinant to proceed to Fumay. Since the mass of his army was pinned down in the north, not much could be done in the south. Moreover, the columns which advanced to Fumay during the day could not get far beyond the Meuse. The only result of all this was the establishment of a German bridgehead on the western bank of the Meuse. The French apparently were retreating from the Meuse, though their rear guards still put up a stiff resistance. An important success seemed to be in the offing for the following day. In order to harass the French by a quick pursuit, the commander of the Third Army on August 24 ordered a continuance of the advance in a general southwestern direction.

This decision was altered on the morning of August 24. The commander of the Second Army dispatched a staff officer to General von Hausen. This officer requested the Third Army to move westward in order to assist the Second Army which was somewhat exhausted by the heavy fighting of August 23. Hausen felt that he was obliged to give Buelow, whom he believed to be hard pressed, all the assistance for which he had asked. He changed his dispositions and thus abandoned the last chance of strategic pursuit. After several hours, German aircraft reported that the enemy forces in front of the Second and Third Army were in full retreat. Consequently, Hausen reverted to his original plan and ordered a new change in the direction of the advance. This general confusion caused much friction and a considerable loss of time. The Third Army on August 24 did not succeed in forcing the retreating enemy to accept battle.

POOR RESULTS OBTAINED

The battle of Namur and Mons yielded only mediocre results for the German army, though the relation of force was not unfavourable for the Germans. The respective dispositions taken on the eve of the battle would have made possible a repetition of the methods applied in the battle of Cannae. On the central front 137 German battalions with 820 cannon fought against 188 French battalions with 748 cannon. Yet on the Meuse, 101 German battalions confronted only 17 French battalions while on the western battlefield, the First Army, in theory at least, could have thrown 120 German battalions with 748 cannon against 52 British battalions with 336 cannon. The Germans had undoubtedly enough strength for smashing both Allied flanks. It was only necessary to use the German forces at the right moment and in the right direction.

The Allies had done nothing to prevent the Germans from

winning a Cannae. Like Terentius Varro, they were ready "to contribute their share to the great objective."

The French Fifth Army under General Lanrezac which proceeded northward along the Sambre, west of Namur, on August 21 was informed by the French High Command that the Germans advanced with strong forces on both banks of the Meuse. The Fifth Army was directed to attack the northermost German units by wheeling around Namur. To the British, who had finished their concentration on August 20, the French High Command suggested that they follow the movements of the Fifth Army by forming, so to speak, the left wing of that French unit.

When on August 21, the Second Army began its attack across the Sambre and when the French cavalry corps under General Sordet was pushed back from the Canal du Centre, General Lanrezac stopped his advance beyond the Sambre. It seemed preferable to him to let the enemy attack across the river and then to strike a strong counter-blow. He considered his positions south of the river as sufficiently strong for such strategy, and failed to recognize that the movements of the German Third Army threatened his right flank. He even reduced the strength of this flank at the Meuse in order to strengthen his positions south of the Sambre. By replacing a whole corps through a reserve division, he virtually opened the door of the Meuse front to the German Third Army. After the evening of August 22 the flank and the rear of the French Fifth Army lay open to German attack.

Two French corps on August 22 had suffered considerable losses in the valley of the Sambre. For the next day, Lanrezac intended with his main forces to remain on the defensive and to undertake only a local offensive with one army corps against the east flank of the German Second Army. Yet when the German crossing of the Meuse south of Dinant was reported, this attack stopped after it had scarcely begun. In other words, Lanrezac ordered the same corps which originally were to fight offensively to protect his flank and rear.

During the evening, General Lanrezac also learned that the

French Fourth Army had been forced to retreat toward Mézières. Besides, Namur had fallen to the Germans. The British had been attacked by heavy odds near Mons.

Directions from the French High Command were lacking. Consequently, the commander of the French Fifth Army decided, on his own responsibility, to retreat to the line Givet-Maubeuge.

The cooperation between the French Fifth Army and the British Expeditionary Force was still less effective than the cooperation between the different German armies. The British Field Marshal, Sir John French, was an entirely independent commander. The French High Command and the Commander of the French Fifth Army could transmit only suggestions, not orders to the British leader, which he was free to accept or to reject.

After the completion of the British concentration on the evening of August 20, the British commander intended to advance in the direction of Mons. He received on August 21 excellent reports which gave him a correct picture of the situation of the German First and Second Army. Marshal French had also ample information of the German strength and knew that his opponents had six corps in the first and five other corps in the second line. Nevertheless, the British Field Marshal, evidently encouraged by French suggestions, persisted in continuing with his offensive operations. The British Army late on August 22 had reached the Canal du Centre between Nimy (north of Mons) and Thulin; the British right flank was still somewhat lagging behind. Incoming information made it clear that the British were going to be attacked by the Germans and that their left flank was particularly menaced.

BRITISH AND FRENCH RETREAT

Marshal French therefore ordered the advance stopped and the present positions held, thus giving the German First Army a good opportunity to outflank the British army during August 23, provided, of course, the Germans had quickly taken the necessary dispositions for such manoeuvre.

The British front on August 23 was strongly attacked. The Germans entered Mons and put the British forces east of that town in a difficult position. The British also lost Jemappes and St. Ghislain.

Despite these reverses, French on August 24 still intended to hold on to his positions. As a consequence, the Germans had a second opportunity to envelop the British army. When on the following night French was informed that Lanrezac had be gun to retreat, he at last also decided to do the same. The British retreat was ordered at the very last minute and some British units had already difficulties in disengaging themselves from the enemy.

We have seen that the German army had a good chance to score a decisive victory at the expense of the British and French on August 23. The Allies, like Terentius Varro, had strengthened their front and weakened their wings. Besides, they had chosen to attack the strongest points of the German positions, thus again imitating the tactics of Terentius Varro. The Allies did not use the British Expeditionary Force as a mobile wing operating independently from the French Fifth Army against the axis of the German advance. To be sure, the British may not have been able to execute such complicated strategy. The mere lengthening of the French front by simply adding the British to the French line facilitated the outflanking of the Allied armies by the Germans.

On the other hand, the presence of strong British forces near Mons surprised the First German Army. Yet the British were not able to exploit this successful surprise because their positions offered no opportunity for effective manoeuvres against the German flanks. Throughout the whole battle, the German Army was able to impose its law on the enemy. It would have been possible to apply Count von Schlieffen's doctrine and to attack the enemy's flanks with the main German forces, provided the necessary orders had been issued in time and energetically carried out. The two British corps were held up by the frontal attack of two German corps. Thus, three German corps and three cavalry divisions were available for at attack on the British flanks. The British could have opposed only one infantry brigade against these strong German forces This brigade, just arrived from England, began to move forward on August 23. The Germans were thus undoubtedly in a position to win a quick and important victory. It is even probable that they would have cut off the British retreat.

TIMOROUS GENERALSHIP

In World War I, envelopment was usually avoided by immediate retreat. Most generals became apprehensive of the security of their flanks and withdrew their forces when a threat against the flanks materialised. During the initial operations in this war, British generalship was still rather clumsy. It is questionable whether the British forces would have escaped from a German pincer-attack. Besides, Marshal French was quite willing to let himself be surprised. He worried so little about the situation on his left flank that as late as the evening of August 23 he intended to remain in his positions, assuming, however, that the French would also continue to hold to theirs.

On the Meuse, German leadership could have taken advantage of equally good opportunities. The German attack south of Dinant took the French completely by surprise. As we know, Clausewitz taught that surprise is the chief means of achieving numerical superiority at the decisive point. By their successful surprise, the Germans had indeed concentrated vastly superior numbers at the Meuse, which was the decisive point of the whole battlefield, though here again their superiority existed only in theory. Had the Germans attacked in greater strength—which was possible—and had they extended their offensive further to the south, the French could not have warded off the threat against their flank and rear. Nor could they have retreated to the south and southwest. The French would have been obliged to accept battle on a reversed front. Large forces would have undoubtedly been encircled by the Germans. The hesitations and the confusion on the part of the German commander prevented the harvesting of the fruits of successful surprise.

It appears that the British and French formations were menaced by an attack on their both flanks. If the Germans had been able to complete their deployment, the Allied forces in northern France would have been eliminated. As it was, the German army made, so to speak, only a feint along the lines of the battle of Cannae. But this feint induced the Allies to retreat.

The following day, the French High Command, again did its best to help the Germans win the decisive victory which had escaped them on August 23. The French High Command was not in agreement with General Lanrezac's decision to break battle and to retreat. In their opinion, an attack of the French Fifth Army could have been successful on August 24. There is little doubt that a French offensive move would have persuaded the British Field Marshal to stay in his positions at Mons and thus to offer his flank to a German blow. Nor can there be any doubt that the strategy devised by the French High Command would have led the French Fifth Army and the British Expeditionary Force to disaster.

GERMAN MOVEMENTS IGNORED

The history of the German advance through Belgium shows that the Germans had good opportunities to deceive their opponents and to surprise them by the disposition and the concentration of their forces, despite that the Allies fought in a country almost entirely inimical to the Germans. An army lighting on its own, or in a friendly, country is always better supplied with information. Still, the French and British ignored the German movements for a considerable period of time.

Up to August 18 the French High Command was not yet sure whether the Germans would operate with strong forces on both sides of the Meuse or concentrate only small forces on the left bank of that river and deliver their main attack against the French Fourth Army. It was not until August 21 that the French Fifth Army received word from the French High Command that the Germans could be expected to launch their main attack in the region between Brussels and Givet.

By that time General Lanrezac already knew that the same German army which had taken Liege had occupied Brussels and that another German army was about to cross the Meuse near Namur. He rightly deduced from these facts that the Germans would soon appear on the Sambre. However, General Lanrezac ignored the situation on the Meuse front south of Namur. He did not know that the Third German army approached the Meuse on both sides of Dinant. Instead, he assumed that only one or two German corps operated in that sector. Besides, he underestimated the total strength of the three German armies which he thought to be composed of nine or ten corps. In reality, the Germans had twelve corps available for their operation on the Sambre and Meuse front while Lanrezac could muster only seven corps, including the British.

The British, up to August 20, remained totally ignorant of the location of their enemy. Until the evening of that day, British cavalry had met with no Germans. On the same day, air reconnaissance observed a German column marching westward through Louvain. The British on August 22 had full information of the German movements.

On the German side the lack of information was even worse. They knew by August 20 that a strong French army was being assembled in the Sambre-Meuse triangle between Charleroi and Dinant. However, many important points remained obscure. On the morning of August 22 the commander of the German Second Army still believed that only weak French forces, chiefly cavalry, stood south of the Sambre. General von Hausen appears to have been ignorant that the French positions opposite the Third German Army on the Meuse were undermanned. His information service failed to inform him of the highly important replacement of a whole French corps by a reserve division, although this movement was carried out in broad daylight. General von Kluck was taken by surprise when British troops appeared before his front. And it took him quite a few hours definitely to convince him that he was opposed by the bulk of the British Expeditionary Force. All in all, none of the commanders of the three German armies got a clear picture of the situation. Every one of them was highly surprised when, on the morning of August 24, the Allied retreat was revealed.

EACH GENERAL HIS OWN JUDGE

The lack of sufficient information of the German commanders was largely responsible for the disappointing outcome of the battle. Each German commander interpreted the general situation according to the particular situation at his own front. The commander of the Third Army was overimpressed by the natural strength of the French Meuse positions near Dinant as well as by the repeated requests of the Second Army to lend assistance for the attack in the Sambre sector. The commander of the Second Army as strongly affected by the violence of the battle south of the Sambre. The Second Army had clashed head-on with enemy forces for equal and at some places even superior strength. Besides, the French positions were covered by the Sambre; Namur and Maubeuge, two big fortresses as yet uncaptured, constituted a virtual threat against the flanks of Bulow's army. It must be admitted that the Second Army was in a difficult position. It is understandable why Bulow exerted his main efforts to secure first of all tactical safety for himself. Overestimating the strength and power of his opponent, he wanted to concentrate all available German units for achieving a tactical victory in his sector. He demanded that the First and Third Army close in with his forces as much as possible, without considering that by doing so he narrowed the German offensive front and hence reduced the possibility of manoeuvre against the enemy flanks. Bulow paid more attention to the tactical situation of his own army than to the strategic opportunities of the whole German force.

The commander of the First Army, on the contrary, thought

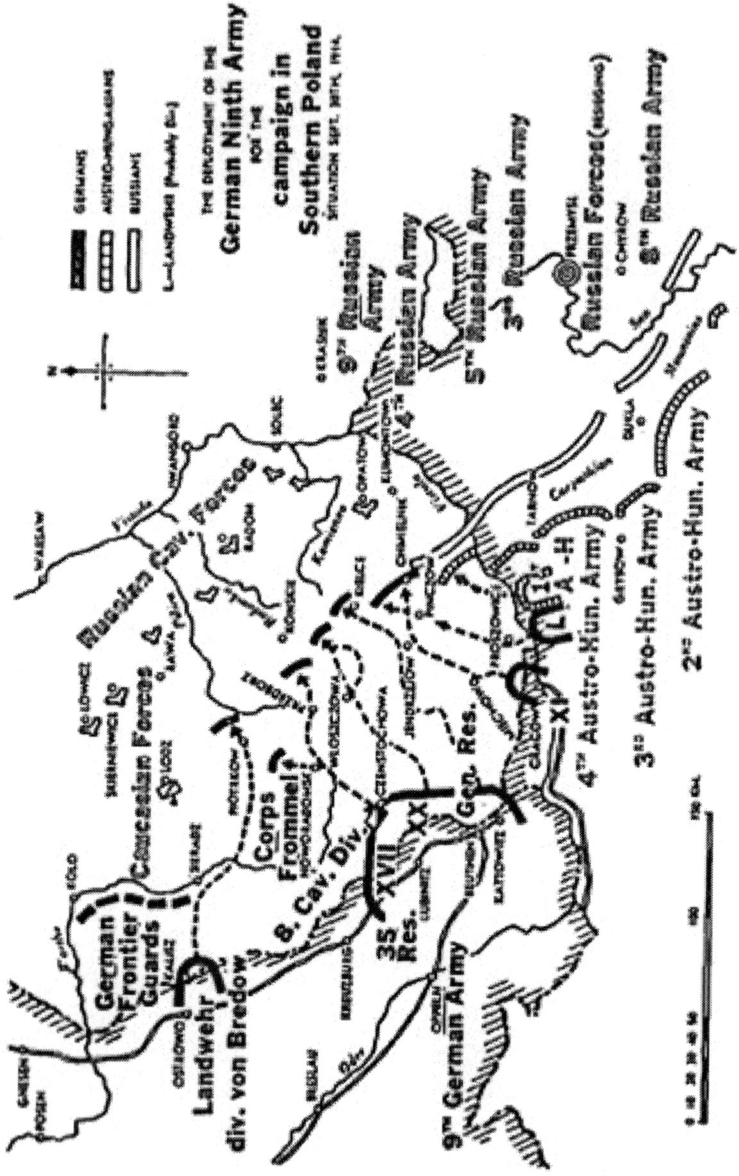
German Ninth Army
campaign in
Southern Poland
Russian Cav. Forces
Caucasian Forces
German Frontier Guards
Landwehr
div. von Bredow
8. Cav. Div.
Corps Frommel
35 Res.
9th German Army
Gd. Res.
4th Austro-Hun. Army
3rd Austro-Hun. Army
2nd Austro-Hun. Army
9th Russian Army
4th Russian Army
5th Russian Army
3rd Russian Army
Russian Forces
8th Russian Army

more in strategic than in tactical terms. However, General von Kluck was guided less by the desire to attack the open flank of the enemy than by anxiety to dispel his uncertainty concerning the location of the British Expeditionary Force. He thus tried to solve two different and more or less incompatible problems.

To command an open and moving flank of the strength of a whole army is a very heavy responsibility. The right combination of boldness and prudence cannot be determined by intellectual reasoning alone. Divination and intuition are likewise necessary. In difficult situations, the intellect of a military leader is less important than his character. Yet he will listen chiefly to reasoned arguments. Flanking and encircling attacks involve heavy risks; a skilful and daring opponent may be able to launch a counterflanking attack against the flanking force.

Prudent leadership is in fundamental contradiction with the idea of annihilation. A prudent general will never be able to surprise his Opponent. This is why Count von Schlieffen Lime and again emphasised audacity and preferred bold solutions for his tactical and strategical exercises. He emphatically warned of prudent solutions which would never lead to a decisive victory. A military decision must be determined by the burning desire to beat the enemy and not by the wish to avoid defeat."

AN IMPORTANT PRINCIPLE

In his last discussion of military problems, he once more drew the attention of his student-officers to the importance of his principle: "It seems that the idea of the battle of annihilation which permeated the strategy of Frederick the Great and Napoleon and which is at the bottom of Moltke's incomparable successes, begins to fall into oblivion and disregard. In the numerous compositions which you handed to me I found mention only twice of the intention to annihilate the enemy. On the contrary, most of your studies are concerned with precautionary measures and do envisage only a slightly energetic blow."

It must be recognised, however, that the German commanders during the battle of Mons could only guess of their opportunities. In war, complete and reliable information about the enemy is always Jacking. Clausewitz even went so far as to assert that three quarters of the facts which one should know in order to make the right decision remain shrouded in uncertainty. He who waits too long for better information risks the loss of a good opportunity. Thucydides' famous saying that good opportunities do not wait is still valid in modern war.

One important lesson must be drawn from the battle of Namur and Mons, namely that a modern battle of annihilation should never be commanded by three commanders of equal rank.

In every war, the absence of one single will was a clear disadvantage. A divided High Command rarely led to great success. It is true that Prince Eugene and Marlborough together won the battles of Hoechstaedt and Malplaquet. This was, however, predominantly due to Eugene's adaptability and personal modesty. Personalities like Eugene are extremely rare among great captains. Most soldiers have it in their blood to stress their independence and object to division of command as well as to subordination which is not based upon the ordinary military hierarchy.

A military duumvirate was still possible in the War of the Spanish succession, but is no longer practical at the present time. Two hundred years ago, armies were small when measured by today's standards. Battles were fought on a terrain of the size of a modern drill-ground. The entire battlefield could be overlooked from a small eminence. Battles did not differ radically from drill movements. If two commanders were agreed upon the general plan for the battle, the divisions of command could hardly interfere with the actual fight.

In this period of mass armies, divided leadership is no longer feasible. The three German commanders had to improvise the function of the German High Command which had eliminated itself. They cannot be reproached if they did not perfectly fulfil their unexpected task. Modern battles cannot be fought with a deteriorated High Command.

The commander-in-chief must be the only commander and every operation must be conducted by a single leader faith absolute authority. For only a leader with ample authority will be capable of mustering the superhuman strength necessary *for commanding a modern battle.*

It may be questionable whether a future war will again begin with lengthy marches to the actual battlefield, as in August, 1914. Probably, a future war will begin under conditions similar to those which at the opening of World War I prevailed on the German-French frontier. Advances in depth will in future occur only after a gap has been opened in frontier fortifications. Consequently, the advance to the battlefield will be but the second act of a future offensive following a victorious struggle for positions near the frontier.[4]

During World War I, many offensives were carried out on the Eastern front through regions not yet affected by the war, such as the advance of the German Ninth Army to the middle Vistula in October, 1914, and the German advance to Lithuania and Curland in the spring of 1915.

CAMPAIGN ON THE VISTULA

The German campaign in the loop of the Vistula in October, 1914, ended undecisively. We propose to examine whether surprise was an important factor in these operations.

General von Conrad on September 1 asked the German High Command to send strong and fresh German forces to the Galician front. He asked for two corps which should move towards Przemysl. The Austrian chief-of-staff expected these German forces to change fundamentally the situation on this front. The German High Command repeatedly discussed the question of German assistance to the Austrian army during the first half of September. It was agreed in principle on September 14 to accede to the

Austrian request. At the same time, it was stipulated that no German troops should be taken from the western front.

A new German army, the Ninth, on September 15, was formed for cooperation with the Austrian forces. In an order of the German High Command, dated September 17, the tasks of this new army were formulated as follows: "To operate independently, although in conjunction with the Austrian High Command, against the flanks and rear of the Russian army group which is in pursuit of the Austrians."

The transportation of the Ninth Army began on the night of September 16-17 in East Prussia. The mass of the Ninth Army was massed in the region of Gleiwitz-Beuthen-Czenstochowa-Lublinitz. One corps was directed to Cracow, and other troops into the sector of Kalisz-Ostrovo. The detrainment began on September 18 and was ended on October 2, when the ammunition supply had arrived. The assembly of the troops on September 28 was begun behind the positions from where their offensive was to be launched.

According to the agreement with General von Conrad, the mass of the German Ninth Army reached the line Chmielnik-Kielce on September 30. The left wing of this German army had already reached the regions west of Konskie, Piotrkow and Novo Radomsk. The German Ninth Army and the Austrian left wing north of the Vistula began to advance on October 1. The mass of the Austrian-Hungarian army south of the Vistula began to move forward on October 4.

The offensive aimed at the two flanks of the Russian forces which, on the left banks of the San and Vistula, occupied a line from Przemysl to south of Ivangorod. The German units had to envelop the Russian northern flank, while the Austrian Second Army in the sector of Przemysl had to outflank the Russian left wing.

This plan had fair chances of giving good results, provided secrecy to the last minute could be maintained. Its chances were dubious in case the deployment of strong German forces north of the upper Vistula and their advance through Poland became prematurely known to the Russians. For the Russians would hardly have permitted the Germans to threaten their right flank without reacting forcefully and speedily.

RADIO MESSAGES UNCIPHERED

In effect, the Russians were quickly informed about the German troop movements in upper Silesia. And this was only natural, since the assembly of the German Ninth Army was not effectively screened by Austrian forces. On the other hand, the Germans and Austrians were equally well informed of the Russian moves. In that territory, secret agents played an important role for both parties. Besides, the Russians still stuck to their habit of not enciphering important radio messages, a habit which already during the battle of Tannenberg proved to be very helpful to the Germans.

The commander of the Russian southwestern front received early intelligence of the appearance of German infantry units on the river Warthe and of the "daily arrival of thirty-seven troop trains" in Czenstochova. He took this information as pretext to protest against the weakening of his right flank which was planned by the new commander of the Russian northwestern front, General Russki, who at that time, envisaged his retreat from the line of the Narev.

The first German units, on September 20, arrived in Czenstochova. The first strategic Russian countermove came on September 22 when the Russian High Command intervened in the dispute between the commanders of the northwestern and southwestern fronts.

In view of a probable German offensive in the direction of the bend of the Vistula, the Russian commander-in-chief, Grand Duke Nicolai Nicolaievitch, on September 22 prohibited the retreat of the northwestern front. At the same time, he promised to re-enforce Russki's left wing near Warsaw by two Siberian corps already *en route*. He also directed the commander of the southwestern front to send three army corps and one cavalry division to Ivangorod. Thus, the Grand Duke had already done much to frustrate the German offensive which had not yet begun.

Nevertheless, the Russians did not yet fully realize the meaning of the German manoeuvre. In particular they failed to understand the unexpected dispatch of German troops to the Austrian front. The Russians had counted or, a German offensive from East Prussia in direction of the Narev.

The Russians should not be blamed for their lack of understanding, for the German High Command did not know just what was the sense of a joint German-Austrian operation on the Austrian left flank. The reasons for which General von Conrad had supported his request for German troops no loner existed; the Russian forces formerly in pursuit of the Austrian Army had already been stopped on the line of the river San. There was no longer any danger of an envelopment of the Austrian fronts.

OFFENCE CHANGED TO DEFENCE

At the time of the German deployment, the Russians had five and one-half cavalry divisions on the left bank of the Vistula. Originally, this force had been assigned the mission of outflanking the retreating Austrians. Yet after the appearance of German troops In southern Poland, this offensive mission was changed into a defensive one. Instead of the previously planned crossing of the Vistula, these cavalry divisions were ordered to remain where they were and to protect and screen the Russian positions north of that important waterway.

On the same day, September 22, when the Russians began to organize the defence of the Vistula position, General von Hindenburg energetically requested the Austrian High Command to send strong Austrian forces to the northern bank of this river. This move would be a necessary complement to the movements of the German Ninth Army and would be indispensable to an effective attack against the Russian flank. On the next day the Austrians promised to dispatch considerable forces across the Vistula.

On the evening of September 24, Russian reconnaissance units established the presence of strong German forces along the line Sieradz-Novi-Radomsk-Miechov. A German prisoner informed the Russians moreover of the arrival of a German corps in the sector Beuthen-Tarnowitz. This corps had formerly been stationed in eastern Prussia.

From this available information, General Ivanov, the commander of the Russian southwestern front deduced—one week before the actual beginning of the German offensive—that the imminent German attack would be directed against the great bend of the Vistula. To counter the German move effectively, he proposed to retreat behind the Vistula, San and Tanev rivers. General Ivanov's plan, however, was badly received by the Grand Duke who still on September 25 expected a German offensive from East Prussia to the south. The Russians had received ample information of the railroad traffic behind the German lines. They were convinced that no strong forces had been sent from France to the eastern front.

The Grand Duke on September 26, discussed the situation with General Ivanov. They decided upon an active defence of the Vistula line and reinforced their units on both sides of the river, placing reinforcements chiefly in the northern and western sectors of the front.

At the same time the Germans learned of the regrouping of the Russian forces. In particular, that the Russian Ninth Army with at least three corps would open a new front on the Vistula west of Krasnik, although mainly with a defensive mission, though this army could develop a big offensive.

The commanders of the German and Austrian armies thus had to acknowledge the impracticability of their original plan. The attack intended against the flank of the southwestern Russian army group was made impossible by the strong forces which the Russians had brought up to cover the threatened areas. It remained dubious whether the Russians would accept battle on the left or the right bank of the Vistula.

RUSSIANS' SUCCESSFUL PARRY

The Russians received final and definite information of the disposition of the German and Austrian forces on September 30, when they discovered in the diary of a slain German officer that of the six German corps which had fought the battle of the Masurian Lakes only two still remained in East Prussia. Thus, the Russian High Command realised that the main German forces were concentrated along the line Lodz-Kielce, while other strong forces were near Cracow and behind the Carpathian mountains. The German concentration between Lodz and Kielce was rightly considered as extremely dangerous. The Russians understood that they had to neutralize this threat by a strong counter-blow and they prepared an attack against the front of the German Ninth Army. They took measures to attack the German left flank by a whole army reinforced by two or three corps. The Russian counter-blow was therefore ready before the German operation had even begun.

When, on October 1, the German Ninth Army began to move forward, a strategic surprise against the Russians in southern Poland was already out of question. The Russians parried effectively every German move and finally imposed their own law on the Germans. At long last, the Germans had no other way out of their difficulties than to retreat into upper Silesia. This unexpected failure of the campaign in southern Poland must be ascribed chiefly to the previous failure to surprise the Russians.

The Germans did not succeed any better with their offensive in Lithuania and Courland in the spring of 1915. The commander of the German eastern front intended by a surprise, offensive to push the Russians back from the Njemen and from Kowno, with the hope that during The operation strong Russian forces could be caught in trap. Precautions were taken to concentrate the German attacking forces only shortly before the zero hour. On the evening of April 26, the German units were ready and on the following night the offensive began. Much had been expected from it. Yet the offensive did not succeed.

The Russians had received timely warning of the German preparations. They frustrated the planned destruction of their troops by methodically retreating before the German advance. Despite their desire, the vastly superior German forces could not catch up with the Russians, although the Russian retreat was by no means quick. Surprise is an essential condition of victory.

Our examples reveal that during World War I the surprise of the enemy during the advance to the battlefield was possible in theory, but could be scarcely achieved in practice. In the present, the difficulties of surprise have become even greater. In particular, the means and methods of reconnaissance have improved. If surprise should be attempted in future, it will be necessary, on one hand, to keep utmost secrecy by improved camouflage and by executing movements only during the night. On the other, the speed of operations must be increased by the use of motorised units hurled against the flanks and the rear of the enemy. But it is essential to exploit a successfully achieved surprise by concentrating strong forces at the point where the decision shall be won. Modern strategists have sinned much too often against the principle of concentration, although this principle has been valid at all times and is now as valid as ever before.[5]

NOTES

1. Klucks halt: The nervousness of the German commanders was due to a cause which is rarely mentioned in German publications, but which was of deceives importance: The size of the German Army and its speed was inadequate for the successful execution of the German war plan. Besides, forced marches had over-strained the troops as well as the staffs. There seems to have been a widespread fear among the German superior officers that a continued advance would necessarily weaken the German army and make their lines so thin that they would not be able to resist a strong counter-attack. Before 1933, the *Militaer-Wochenblatt* repeatedly declared that, if the Germans had not lost the Battle of the Marne, they would have lost the Battle of the Seine.

   The insufficient strength of the German offensive wing was the main reason why the Germans did not attempt to envelop Paris, but to by-pass it in the east, a movement which enabled Galliéni to attack the German flank.

   Many German writers have criticised the German war plan of 1914 on the ground that the German offensive wing was not Made stronger. That, in particular, two army corps which had been created after Schlieffen's retirement should have been used on the German right wing. This theoretical view however, is hardly borne out by the facts. The Germans had actually used all the troops which they could possibly transport through Belgium. There is a limit to any concentration, which limit is usually determined by the existing transport facilities.

2. Crossing of the Meuse: During the Battle of Flanders in World War II German armoured units which had reached the Meuse more quickly than expected, renounced organizing a systematic crossing, but improvised a swift crossing in order to keep up with the speed of operation.
3. Reliable Information: The facts related above conclusively show the necessity of systematically deceiving and confusing the enemy. It has been reported that during 1942 the Germans added a Section for *Irrefuebrung* (that is, for confusing and misleading the enemy) to their General Staff. There is no reason to assume that the Germans in August, 1914, were confused by mere accident. On the contrary, the British had put an elaborate scheme for misleading their enemy into operation. They were successful because they had discovered the German espionage system in England and used, or rather abused, it without knowledge on the part of the Germans. During the first days of the war they transmitted to Germany the information that the British army would not leave Great Britain. Later, they spread false information of the size of the British Expeditionary Force and the points of disembarkment. During the critical phase of the operations in August 1914, they made the Germans fear a British attack from Ostende, that is to say, against rear and flank of the German First Army. Moreover, they spread the rumour that strong Russian forces, recently landed in England, would attack the Germans in the same region.
4. Approach to battle: The modern defence organisation of extreme depth does prevent big battles at the frontier. In order to forstall surprises, the defender forces the attacker to advance deeply into enemy territory and to reveal the articulation of the offensive army. Consequently, surprises during approach are still possible.
5. Concentration: General Erfurth's examples show that surprise has become more difficult for the attacking, but not necessarily for the defending, army. It is possible to let the offensive army advance and to trap it according to a preconceived plan. In August, 1914, the French intended to let the Germans advance beyond the Sambre and to attack the German units south of that river with superior forces. In October, 1914, the Russians planned to permit a German advance from eastern Prussia to the east and to counter-attack the German rear flank from the direction of Warsaw. However, advancing armies did not lose all possibilities of surprise. If an offensive army will accomplish surprise also during approach, it is only necessary to screen effectively the main concentration of force.

V

Battle

If surprise is really indisperisable to a battle of annihilation, we should *a priori* assume that surprise played an important role in the battle of Tannenberg. For this was a most perfect example of a modern battle of annihilation. The German official history of World War I goes so far as to rank Tannenberg higher than all other battles of envelopment in history and rates it above the classical model of Cannae itself.

The greatness of that German victory is by no means diminished if we acknowledge that faulty Russian leadership considerably facilitate the task of the German command. The outcome of that battle was dependent as well on the mediocrity of Russian generalship as on the high quality of that of the German. The main merit of the. German command consisted in having discovered, and exploited, the errors of the opponent, thus multiplying the consequences of the accomplished strategic surprise.

The Germans in August, 1914, were favoured by all the advantages of the battlefield in East Prussia, while the disadvantages of terrain operated against the Russians. In addition, the staff of the German Eighth Army read all the important Russian radio-messages and thereby had exact and complete knowledge of the enemy's intentions. There is hardly a historical precedent for this. The commanders of the two Russian armies on August 25 informed each other by radio of the disposition of

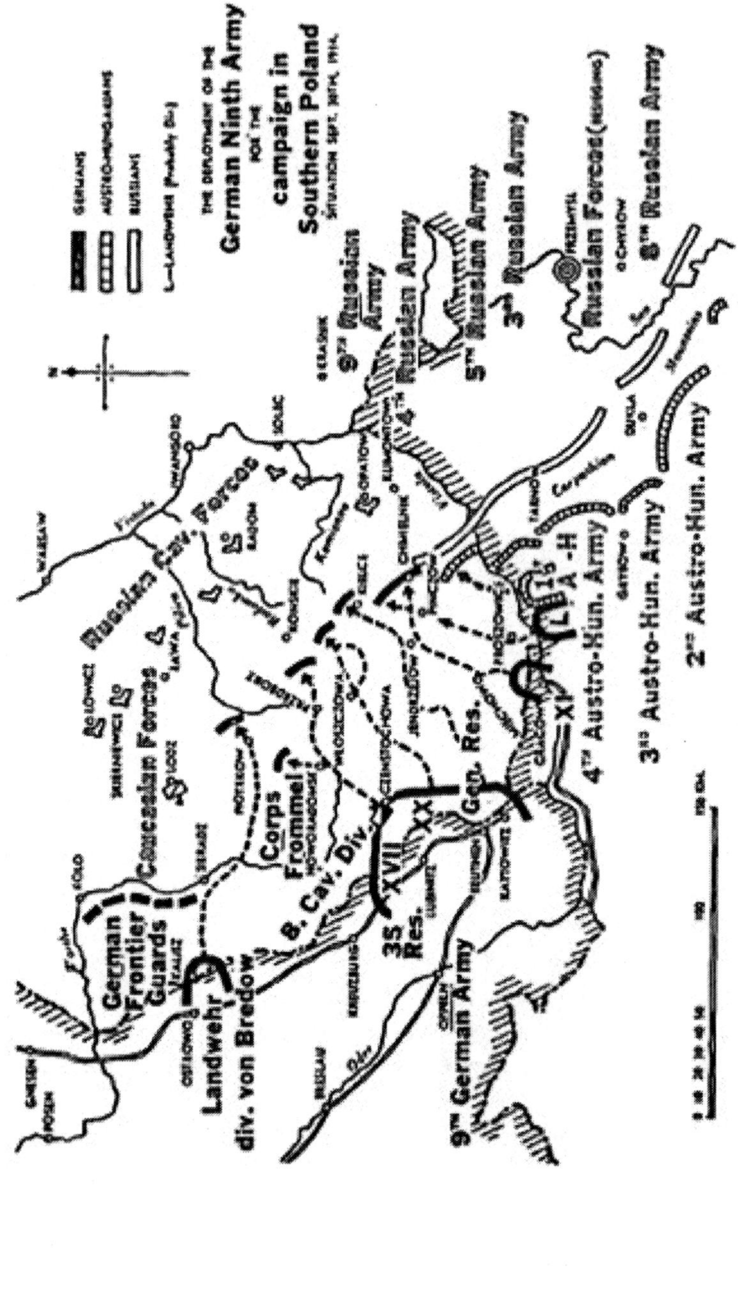
German Ninth Army
campaign in
Southern Poland
Russian Cav. Forces
Caucasian Forces
German Frontier Guards
Landwehr
div. von Bredow
Corps Frommel
8. Cav. Div.
35 Res.
XVII
XX
Gd. Res.
XI
9th German Army
4th Austro-Hun. Army
3rd Austro-Hun. Army
2nd Austro-Hun. Army
9th Russian Army
4th Russian Army
5th Russian Army
3rd Russian Army
Russian Forces
8th Russian Army

their forces and the objective of their movements. The Germans intercepted these radiograrns and thus were able to base their own decisions upon invaluable complete information. Hence a surprise move could be attempted under exceptionally favourable conditions. The "Cannae of Eastern Prussia" was the result of a combination of merit, luck and surprise-methods on the one side and of mistakes, omissions and ill luck on the other.

In the preceding battle of Gumbinnen the Russians had suffered severe losses, They therefore did not expect the German retreat which they discovered early in the morning of August 21. They were somewhat suspicious because they did not understand why the Germans retreated for a second time, inasmuch as they had delivered a serious blow to the Russian army. (On August 17, German forces had retreated after a successful engagement near Stallupoenen.) The Russian command expected the Germans to make a new stand on previously fortified positions behind the Angerapp river. During the next day, however, they found that the Germans had evacuated this position.

Thereupon, the commander of the Russian Army of the Niemen assumed that the Germans were retreating behind the Vistula, although he was prepared for strong German rearguard actions and delaying tactics in prepared positions. After two days of rest, the Army of the Niemen began its advance to the west.

RUSSIAN COMMANDER'S BELIEF

When General Shilinski, commander of the Russian northwestern front, received information of the evacuation of the Angerapp line, lie became convinced that the Germans were retreating behind the Vistula. Since the German civilian population began to flee, he expected the total evacuation of East Prussia, with the exception of the fortress of Koenigsberg which was the apparent objective of strong retreating German forces. In the belief that the Russian Army of the Narev was being opposed by weak German forces, General Shilinski directed this army to cut the retreat of these German units which were being pushed back by the Army of the Niemen. He hoped to annihilate them before they could make their escape across the Vistula.

In the night of August 23-24, after an engagement in the Lahna-Orlau sector, the German XX Corps withdrew its left flank to a position on both sides of a lake near Muehien. This move led the commander of the Russian Army of the Narev erroneously to believe that the whole XXI Corps had retreated in the direction of Osterode. General Samsonov thereupon decided to concentrate his army further west and to march forward to the Allenstein-Osterode line, instead of continuing his former advance toward Sensburg-Allenstein. To protect his right flank, he left his six corps and one cavalry division near Bischofsburg.

General Samsonov on August 25, saw that his interpretation of the German disposition had been incorrect. He now believed the XIX German Corps to stand near Allenstein or Osterode, the XVII south of Gildenburg, and other German forces farther west of this area. This new error was due to the concentration of German landweht and reserve formations west of Gildenburg. For the first time Samsonov vaguely suspected that those German units which some days ago had fought near Gumbinnen had been moved by rail to another sector. He remained entirely ignorant of the presence of strong German forces east of Gildenburg, but expected a German advance from the general direction of Thorn on the Vistula, that is to say, far from the southwest of Gildenburg.

The attack of the German Eighth Army on the left flank of the Narev Army did not catch the Russians by surprise. General Samsonoff awaited the German attack with confidence and was convinced that the Russian forces concentrated in the region of Usdau would be strong enough for any emergency. These Russian troops had two days in which to take appropriate defence measures. Yet the Russian leaders still had a wrong picture of the German dispositions in the Muehien and Hohenstein-Atlenstein-Osterode sectors.

GERMAN MOVEMENTS MISSED

As a matter of fact, the German attack on the eastern flank of the Narev Army developed a complete surprise to the Russians which they themselves had facilitated. For their reconnaissance units failed to notice most important German movements, in particular the march of the XVII German corps from the north to the sector of Bischofsburg. This march was a rather remarkable military exploit since the German unit marched along the front of the Russian Army of the Niemen, thus offering an open flank to the enemy. It is still more remarkable that the Russians remained ignorant of this movement and completely disregarded any possible danger that might threaten the Narev Army from the north. On the night of August 25-26, the Russian VI Corps still stood near Bischofsburg, without even taking the precaution to reconnoitre the areas farther north. The Russians, therefore, learned of the German advance only on the morning of August 26, when they were surprised and defeated near Gross-Boessau. This setback forced the Russians to retire in the direction of Ortelsburg. This local retreat opened the way for a German attack against the flank and rear of the Narev Army whose commander for a long time remained in total ignorance of that important development. Not in the least did he imagine that the German units which he supposed to be west of Usdau had actually advanced behind the flank and rear of his army, let alone that they were about to begin the very attack essential to winning a battle of annihilation, namely, an attack against his flanks.

General Samsonov learned of the Russian defeat near Gross-Boessau around noon on August 27. In the evening of the same day he received the additional bad news that the Russian 1st Corps had been beaten near Usdau and was falling back on Mlava.

The Russian commander did not immediately realize the full implications of these defeats on his both flanks. He gave orders to continue with the attack during the next day. It is true that on the morning of this day he at last understood how disastrous his decision had been in his last report which he dispatched to his superiors in the morning of August 28, he characterised the situation of his army as "extremely, dangerous." Despite this correct appreciation, the retreat of the Narev Army was not ordered until the evening of August 28, much too late to save the mass of the Russian forces.

MISSION OF THE RUSSIANS

At the outbreak of the war, the northwestern group of the Russian army had been charged "to annihilate the German units in East Prussia" or to cut them off from Koenigsberg and the Vistula. The Russians therefore had to operate on outer lines. In our discussion of the battle of Mons and Namur, we have already pointed out that the coordination, of the movements of different and geographically separated units constitutes the main difficulty of such an operation. The commander of the Russian northwestern front was not equal to this admittedly difficult task. The operations were executed in vast spaces and he was unable to get a correct view of them. Besides, he lacked the energy which is so necessary for simultaneously conducting large-scale operations on different fronts.

Nor had the commanders of the two Russian armies the correct appreciation of the situations involved, thus failing at a similar task which, during the same weeks, also proved to be beyond the capacities of the German leaders on the Sambre and Meuse.

If the Russian generals had been in possession of better information, a quick advance on the part of General von Rennenkampf and a cautious defensive on the part of General Samsonov would have avoided the catastrophe of Tannenberg. In this battle the Russians possessed huge numerical superiority. Approximately 485,000 Russians were confronted by only 73,000 Germans of the Eighth Army. However, General Shilinski, as a disciple of Terentius Varro, did not use his superiority to concentrate overwhelming forces at decisive points, for the simple reason that he did not believe that the Germans would accept a

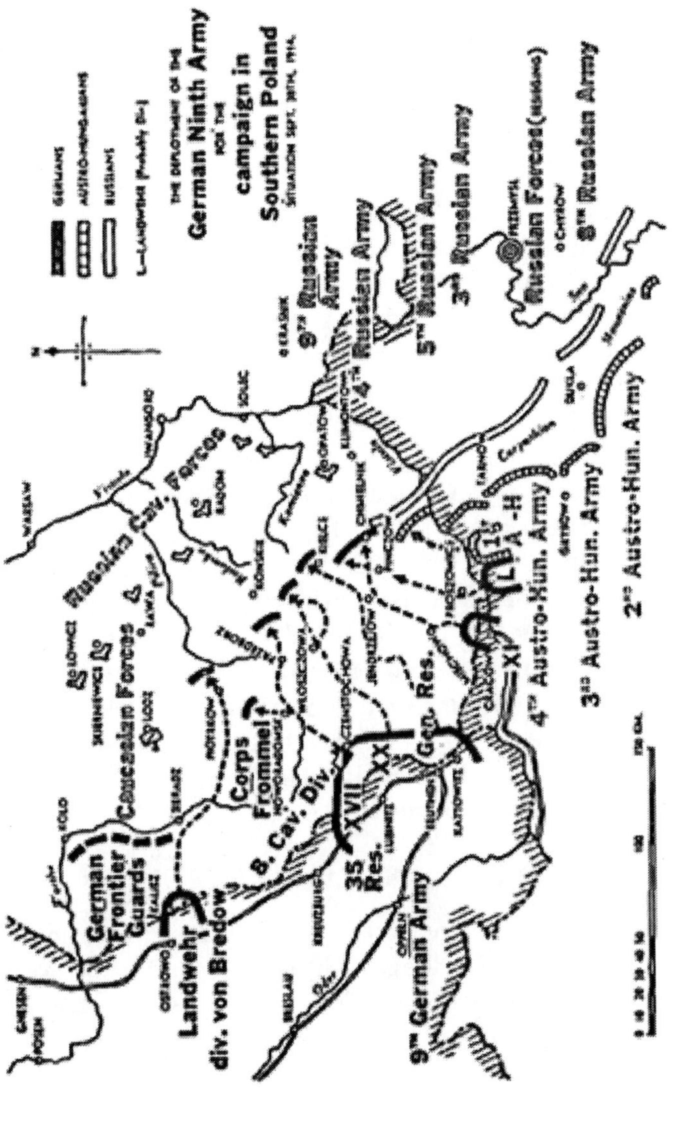
German Ninth Army
campaign in Southern Poland
9th German Army
Landwehr
div. von Bredow
German Frontier Guards
Caucasian Forces
Russian Cav. Forces
Corps Frommel
8. Cav. Div.
35 Res.
XVII
XX
Gd. Res.
XI
4th Austro-Hun. Army
3rd Austro-Hun. Army
2nd Austro-Hun. Army
9th Russian Army
4th Russian Army
5th Russian Army
3rd Russian Army
Russian Forces
8th Russian Army

big battle cast of the Vistula. After the battle of Gumbinnen, General Shilinski considered the German Eighth Army as already beaten and mentally prepared himself for the operations supposedly imminent on the Vistula. Underestimation of the opponent is always highly dangerous. The Germans were lucky to have in General Shilinski an opponent who split his armies and dispersed his forces for secondary operations. That is the main reason why General Samsonoff had to light the battle of Tannenberg alone. During the decisive operations, 153,000 Germans, 296 machine guns and 728 cannon were opposed by 191,000 Russians, 384 machine guns and 612 cannon, although they could have been opposed by at least twice that number. The Germans possessed one superiority only. Leadership. It enabled them to strike decisively at the vulnerable points of the enemy. Incidentally, Tannenberg is the only battle of World War I in which separate advances of different armies and an attack from two independent fronts led to victory.[1]

Originally, the German Eighth Army's mission was only defensive. The Germans had practically no chance to hold the German territory east DI the Vistula unless they separated the different Russian armies and defeated them successively. For that purpose the dispositions of the German forces had to remain hidden from the enemy. In point of fact, German leadership was able thoroughly to deceive the Russians on all important German dispositions and movements.[2]

SPEED IN INNER LINE MOVES

The German Army operated on inner lines. Since the enemy cannot be deceived for long, such operations must be executed with the utmost speed. But once the offensive has begun, the enemy receives the information he needs by the very movements of the attacking troops. Consequently, surprise can only be utilised during the preparatory phases of the attack. "Almost the only advantage of attack," says Clausewitz, is the possibility of surprise with the first blow." The German forces that won the engagement of Gross-Boessau delivered such a first blow. Their attack came suddenly and was pressed home without giving respite to the enemy. Thus it led not only to the defeat of the Russian VI Corps, but eventually to the annihilation of the entire Russian Army of the Narev.

Several other attempts were made during World War I to defeat a numerically superior enemy by an offensive on inner lines. But a complete victory like that of Tannenberg was not accomplished a second time.

Some similar attempts led to ordinary victories, as at the battle of Hermannstadt. But other attempts repeatedly miscarried, as the Rumanian offensive west of Bucharest in the winter of 1916. In the battle of the Arges, the Rumanian High Command intended to beat the Army of the Danube and to drive it back across the river before the right wing of the German Ninth Army under the command of General Kuehne could intervene. The Rumanian forces formerly entrusted with the mission of defending the Danube and a *masse de manoeuvre* constituted for the same operation together had to take the offensive against the Army of the Danube of the Central Powers. The three divisions of the Rumanian right wing had to operate in the direction of Draganescii, while one division and one infantry-brigade of the Rumanian left wing had to attack in the direction of Giurgiul. The Rumanian First Army had to protect the *masse de manoeuvre* offensive against the German units under General Krafft. Between the left wing of the Army of the Danube and the right wing of General Kuehne's forces was a wide gap, which apparently favoured the intentions of the Rumanian commander, General Presan. The Rumanian High Command hoped that on receiving the news of a defeat of the Danube Army, General Kuehne would stop and possibly retreat. They underestimated the danger which menaced the Rumanian forces from Kuehne's group. Consequently, they failed to protect the area between the Rumanian First Army and the Rumanian *masse de manoeuvre* with sufficient forces However, the arrival of several Russian divisions

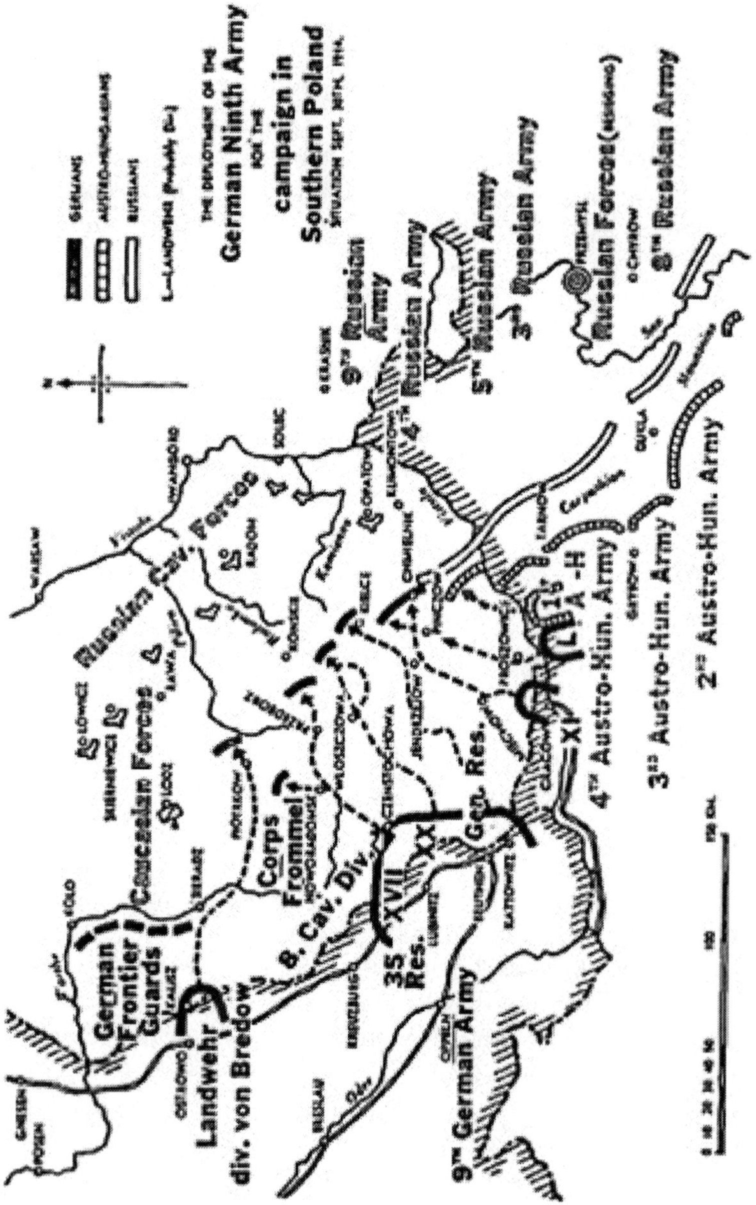
German Ninth Army
campaign in
Southern Poland
Russian Cav. Forces
Caucasian Forces
German Frontier Guards
Landwehr
div. von Bredow
9th German Army
35 Res.
XVII
8. Cav. Div.
Corps Frommel
XX
Gd. Res.
XI
1st A.-H.
4th Austro-Hun. Army
3rd Austro-Hun. Army
2nd Austro-Hun. Army
9th Russian Army
4th Russian Army
5th Russian Army
3rd Russian Army
Russian Forces
8th Russian Army

and of one Rumanian division on the battlefield was imminent. In the opinion of General Presan, these reinforcements would give the Rumanians numerical superiority even in case General Kuehne should continue to advance, after a defeat of the Army of the Danube.

Both opponents lacked sufficient information about each other. Foggy weather made air reconnaissance difficult. The advance of Kuehne's forces was effectively screened by the cavalry corps under General Schmettow. On the whole, the German leaders• had the trump cards in their hands and were in a more favourable situation for achieving surprise than the Rumanians, although the Rumanians, too, tried to surprise their enemy. In effect, the German commanders ignored the fact that forces, of the left flank of the Rumanian *masse de manoeuvre* advanced southward. The southern move, according to Presan's plan, was the most decisive one; it was frustrated, although only in the last hour, when most unexpectedly General Kuehne appeared on the focal sector of the battlefield. Thus, the Rumanian surprisers became the surprised.

LUCK AN ELEMENT

It must be admitted that in this battle the Central Powers were favoured by luck. The headquarters of a Rumanian division which fought on the open flank of the *masse de manoeuvre* had on December 1, been effectively bombed by German aircraft. Consequently, the leadership of this key division became wholly insufficient. On the same day, General von Falkenhayn, commander of the German Ninth Army, gained full knowledge of the Rumanian battle-plan by the seizure of a written order carried by two Rumanian staff-officers who were taken prisoner. To this moment, Falkenhayn had been entirely ignorant of the Rumanian intentions, but after a thorough analysis of the captured orders he realised that General Kuehne's forces were in an exceptionally favourable position not only to parry a dangerous Rumanian blow against the left wing of his Army of the Danube, but also to hit the enemy strongly and offensively at a decisive point. For the Rumanians, while attacking, opened themselves to attack on their flank and rear. Falkenhayn, therefore, ordered General Kuhne to hurry to the battlefield.

Incidentally, before the capture of the two staff-officers, another Rumanian order had fallen into German hands. This was an order from General Presan himself, dated November 29 and addressed to the division on the open flank of the *masse de manoeuvre*. The order contained ample information of the Rumanian plan and in particular of the mission of the *masse de manoeuvre*. Yet, the staff of the cavalry division which came into its possession apparently failed to transmit this valuable document to General von Falkenhayn.

Such incidents are typical and inavoidable in a war with mass-armies. Every student of World War I will know many other examples of the kind. Important orders, even those emanating from the highest military authorities, were captured by he opposing army during practically every big operation. In former times, operational orders were seldom lost to the enemy. This, particular danger to secrecy arose under modern conditions, when it became necessary to multiply important orders because numerous persons must know them. There is hardly a way of dispensing with the multiplication of orders, although this will certainly continue to be the source of difficulty.

Care should be taken to inform subordinate commanders only of the most necessary details and to reveal to them only those points which they must know for accomplishing their particular tasks. The enemy should be unable to deduce the whole plan from a single captured order. To give orders in such a way is certainly a laborious process, but the additional troubles which the staff must incur when editing such orders will undoubtedly be worth while. The orders for the Rumanian First Army carried by the two captured staff-officers contained the orders for all divisions of the *masse de manoeuvre*. This, of course, was unnecessary. Since he advance of the open wing of the *masse de manoeuvre* and its reinforcement by a division from the First Army clearly constituted a heavy risk, as do all marches along the front of the opponent, it was of extreme importance to keep these movements as secret as possible. Yet they were mentioned in the captured documents.

TRANSYLVANIAN CAMPAIGN

The campaign of the German Ninth Army in Transylvania began with a surprise. In September, 1916, the Rumanian army stood in a semicircle around the units of the Central Powers in Transylvania, threatening to annihilate them by concentric attack. The situation was similar to that in which the Austrian. Hungarian Army found itself on the Russian southwestern front in the summer of 1914. The Rumanians were numerically much stronger than the forces of the Central Powers. Yet in order to attack they would have been obliged to travel over several mountain-passes and to divide their forces. Thus, the Central Powers could find a chance successively to beat the different parts of the Rumanian army.

To avoid the danger of a Rumanian concentric attack on the German Ninth Army, a German offensive had to be undertaken against the westernmost Rumanian units. General von Falkenhayn decided to strike his first blow against the Rumanian forces near Hermannstadt. He estimated the Rumanians at twice the number of his own force. This, of course, ruled out a frontal attack, for by attacking frontally, General von Falkenhayn would have had no troops left for an operation against the Rumanian flanks and would have run the risk of being attacked himself on his own wings by superior forces.

General von Falkenhayn was informed that, contrary to expectation, the mountains of Cibina could be negotiated by strong detachments, comparatively speaking. If it was possible to advance through these mountains towards the Red Tower Pass, the enemy could be outflanked and his only supply road cut. If this was done, there was a good chance that a frontal attack would also be successful, despite numerical inferiority.

General von Falkenhayn did not plan the battle of Hermannstadt as a battle of single or double encirclement. Instead, he attempted to combine an attack against the enemy's only supply line with a rather reckless frontal attack.

Falkenhayn on September 20 discussed his plan with his commanding generals. General Krafft von Dellmensingen was directed to prepare the attack of Alpine troops through the mountains of Cibina Two days later the mountain troops began to move while other German forces were being concentrated north of Hermannstadt.

General von Falkenhayn intended to launch his attack on September 26. A whole corps was to move forward on both sides of Hermannstadt in the general direction of the Red Tower Pass. By the same date, it was expected that the Alpine detachments would approach the pass, and also attack. German cavalry units, supported by Austro-Hungarian infantry, were directed to divert from the battlefield the Rumanian Second Army which had taken up positions east of Hermannstadt. For an intervention of the Rumanian Second Army would have endangered the whole position of the German Ninth Army.

MOUNTAIN OPERATIONS

The crux of Falkenhayn's plan depended upon whether the Alpine detachment would arrive in time in the enemy's rear and would be able effectively to close the Red Tower Pass. True enough, the Rumanians were surprised by the unexpected raid of these troops across mountains over six thousand feet high, using mule-tracks and stony paths as roads. The commander of the Rumanian First Army, General Culcer, had given orders to watch the mountains of Cibina, yet the officer in command of this front, who did not believe in the practicability of an enemy thrust through these inhospitable mountains, had recalled all guards to reinforce his positions near Hermannstadt. The history of war offers many examples of a sector which is reputedly not negotiable being passed by strong forces and thus used for surprising the enemy. Some Rumanian guards were still in the mountains when the first Germans appeared. One Rumanian position fell to the advanced guards of a Bavarian brigade, but its garrison escaped. Rumanian shepherds also informed the Rumanian command of the German advance, but the Rumanian commander whose attention was concentrated on other operations, did not consider these reports as important. Some types of military commanders prefer to believe in their own intuition rather than in reliable intelligence. Only one battalion and some guns were diverted for the protection of the Red Tower Pass; another battalion was dispatched to protect the regions west of the pass. These two battalions were attacked the next day by the German mountain troops.

At long last, the Rumanian commander realised the situation and hurriedly dispatched reinforcements to the pass. On September 27 further Rumanian reinforcements arrived at the southern exit of the pass. They immediately counter-attacked through the pass as well as through the mountains farther west, while additional reinforcements arrived from the north.

The German units were much too weak effectively to close the pass and to defend many miles of the pass road against an enemy, by now numerically superior and trying his utmost to reopen his only supply line. Besides, the supplying of the German detachment through the mountains was extremely difficult. The Germans in the pass were soon in a critical situation. They were unable definitely to disrupt the enemy's communications, although they effectively disordered them. Falkenhayn's plan was not a complete success, but this menace against the rear and the Red Tower Pass communications of the Rumanians considerably helped the Germans in the battle of Hermannstadt.

Falkenhayn was more successful with his plan to keep the Second Rumanian Army far from the battlefield. The Rumanian High Command and the commander of the Rumanian Second Army realised the difficulties of the First Army too late. During the afternoon of September 27 the Second Army was ordered to move to the west and to begin a powerful westward offensive which, at first, made good progress. But on September 29 the right wing of the Rumanian army was stopped and finally beaten back. Other Rumanian forces on both banks of the river Alt could make but little progress against German cavalry and were unable to intervene in the battle of Hermannstadt. On the other hand, the units of the Rumanian First Army which had fought north of the Red Tower Pass were exhausted and had already begun to retreat.

As a result of the incomplete control of this pass by the German mountain troops, the Rumanian retreat succeeded, although the Rumanians lost most of their vehicles. Too, the morale of their troops was seriously impaired by this operation.

FORCES TOO WEAK FOR TACK

Falkenhayn's plan to cut off the Rumanian communications near Hermannstadt and to encircle strong Rumanian forces failed. True, the Rumanian commanders had been surprised by the unexpected dash of the mountain units through the mountains of Cibina. But the German detachment was too weak for its task. It was not strong enough at the beginning of the operation, let alone after the Rumanians had been reinforced.

We remember that, according to Clausewitz, surprise should be the means to achieve local numerical superiority. An operation which had not been expected by the opponent is only effective if undertaken by really superior forces. The degree of numerical superiority of the forces executing the surprise move must be determined by the opportunity to reinforce speedily, and also by the ability of the opponent to bring up reinforcements.

In the battle of Hermannstadt both parties, numerically speaking, were more or less equal, although the Central Powers had vast superiority in artillery. It was probably impossible to throw stronger forces against the Red Tower Pass. A decisive victory was therefore beyond Falkenhayn's powers and he was unable to harvest all the Profits from his successful surprise.

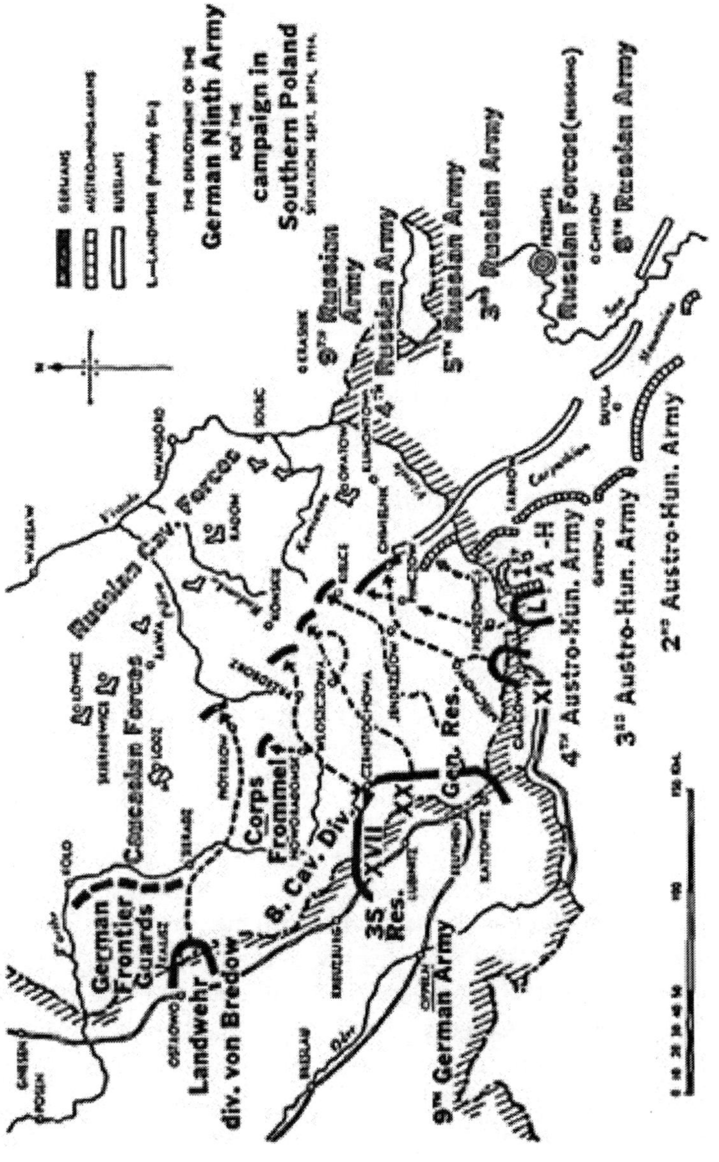
German Ninth Army
campaign in
Southern Poland
German Frontier Guards
Landwehr
div. von Bredow
Caucasian Forces
Russian Cav. Forces
Corps Frommel
8. Cav. Div.
35 Res.
XVII
XX
Gen. Res.
XI
4th Austro-Hun. Army
3rd Austro-Hun. Army
2nd Austro-Hun. Army
9th German Army
9th Russian Army
4th Russian Army
5th Russian Army
3rd Russian Army
Russian Forces
8th Russian Army

Nevertheless, the daring move through the Cibina mountains facilitated the frontal attack and made the Rumanian retreat very difficult. The Rumanian First Corps was thoroughly beaten in this battle. But the German forces which operated against the enemy's rear were too weak to achieve the annihilation of their opponent.

In his study on the Battle of Cannae, Count von Schlieffen emphasised that a battle of annihilation was rarely won by inferior forces, If the enemy's numerical superiority is too great, his front cannot be attacked and no forces can be spared for a flanking operation. In such a case, the only expedient left is *to launch the main attack against the flank*, or, if possible, against the rear and to push the enemy against an unpassable natural obstacle and to outflank him after he has been immobilised. In that way Frederick the Great once tried to win a battle of annihilation against an army twice as strong as his. But in his time, the envelopment of the enemy was a difficult undertaking. Unless the turning movement remains a secret to the enemy, its success is doubtful; If the enemy has time to take appropriate counter-measures, the flanking manoeuvre must fail. And only if secrecy can be combined with speed, is surprise possible.

During World War I strategic envelopment was repeatedly attempted. We will examine sonic of these attempts in order to determine just what role surprise played in them.

Before and during the battle of the Masurian Lakes both sides had incomplete knowledge of the impending movements of the enemy. The Germans were no longer assisted by Russian radio messages in plain language.

The commander of the German Eighth Army was under the impression that the Russian Army of the Niemen prepared for a long stand northwest of the Masurian Lakes. Yet the possibility of offensive moves on the part of the Russians could not be ruled out. The exact strength of the enemy was unknown. In particular, the Germans disregarded the distribution of the Russian forces east and south of the Masurian Lakes and the question of whether reinforcements were approaching. As it so often happens the

Germans overestimated the Russian strength, believing that they were opposed by twenty infantry divisions. In reality, General von Rennenkampf, who in the beginning of September had sixteen and one-half infantry divisions and five and one-half cavalry divisions, began the battle with only fourteen infantry divisions.

FLANK AND FRONT ATTACK

The main Russian forces stood between the Kurische Haff in the north and Lake Mauer in the south. A mere frontal attack against their strong positions did not offer promising prospects. An enveloping movement against the Russian northern flank, which was protected by the Baltic was, for geographical reasons, out of question. The German commander, therefore, decided to combine a frontal attack with an attack against the Russian southern flank. The difficult terrain south of Loetzen, however, made a flanking manoeuvre extremely complicated. The numerous lakes in this sector necessitated a division of the German attacking forces, so that the Russians could find an opportunity to fall upon the German units piecemeal. Those German troops which had to advance south of the lakes were particularly in danger of being attacked by strong Russian units from the area of Lonsza and Grodno.

During the early phases of the battle, the German command apprehended a Russian counter-attack on the German northern flank, although, with our present knowledge of the situation, this fear is hard to understand. For in this case the Russians would have been obliged to evacuate very strong positions and to attack the German forces supported from the fortress of Koenigsberg. However, the German command was justified in taking precautions. An army concentrating the bulk of its forces against one of the enemy flanks always risks a heavy counter-attack from the enemy's other flank. These apprehensions were strengthened by the report of German flyers, according to which the Russians had concentrated large forces far behind their northern flank. The German leaders, therefore, decided to reinforce their left wing Yet it proved to be impossible to divert units from the right to the left flank because the right wing had already advanced too far to the east. This impossibility of reinforcing the left wing at the expense of the right flank was very fortunate for the Germans, for they saw themselves compelled to resort to a ruse of war which not only deceived the Russians into taking faulty positions, but also enabled the. Germans to achieve a successful surprise. It was particularly important to prevent a Russian attack on the German left flank. The German radio on September 7 transmitted a message *en clair* suggesting the arrival of two corps from the western front behind the German left wing.

The exact timing of the German frontal attack with the attack against the Russian flank proved to be a major difficulty. It was hard to tell just bow long the crossing of the lake sector would last, since the terrain offered good possibilities for delaying defensive action by even weak forces. In point of fact, the enveloping movement was too slow for a decisive German victory against the Russian Army of the Niemen.

The battle began on September 8 with the capture of the Russian advanced positions. The main frontal attack was to begin on September 9, yet the speed of its execution was to be timed with the operations against the Russian flank. The lake sector was crossed during September 6 and 7; the German troops had been opposed only by weak Russian forces. Serious opposition had been encountered only on the right flank, but had been overcome.

On the evening of September 9, the German right flank had arrived near Lyck and in the zone of Kruglanken-Possessern. The German command had the impression that the flanking operation proceeded according to plan, but thought that the capture of the Russian main positions would require a major effort. It seemed advisable to postpone the main frontal attack until the German flank had advanced still farther.

AN UNEXPECTED EVACUATION

To the great surprise of the German leaders, the Russians

evacuated their main positions on September 10. This complete and unexpected change was not immediately comprehensible. In view of the strength of the Russians the German command did not dare to begin a swift pursuit. Instead, they ordered a limited advance and strongly admonished the troops to be cautious.

Only after Rennenkampfs retreat had clearly been established by air reconnaissance was a quicker pursuit ordered, yet it did not get under way before September 11.

How did the Russian leaders interpret the German strategy before and during this battle? Still influenced by memory of the catastrophe of Tannenberg, the Russians were uncertain whether the Germans would turn against the Army of the Niemen or that of the Narev. They also considered the possibility of a German thrust against Warsaw which, after the arrival of German forces from the western front, was certainly within the realm of possibility. The Russian press by August 30 had already reported this important German troop movement from the western to the eastern front.

Originally, General von Rennenkampf planned to fight defensively and to hold his strong natural positions behind the line of the Deinie-Alle-Omet rivers and to cover his left flank by the Masurian lakes. He expected a German attack in the vicinity of Loetzen, but not a flanking movement farther south which turned around the region of the lakes. He concentrated his reserves behind his northern flank, fearing German amphibious operations across the Haff and perhaps by the Baltic. On September 7 to his surprise-he learned of the German movement to the east along the southern frontier of East Prussia. Realizing that the Germans were attempting to envelop his weak southern flank, he gave orders to attack strongly on a broad front the open flank of the wheeling Germans.

RENNENKAMPF'S IRRESOLUTION

On the same day, however, the Russians received the German radio-message about the alleged arrival of two German corps behind the northern flank. Rennenkampf became irresolute and could not make up his mind whether he should accept battle or withdraw. In the hope that the Germans had made available for their flanking manoeuvre only weak forces, he finally resolved to make a stand.

The hope of stopping the envelopment attack of the German right wing by a strong attack against its open side soon proved vain. The Germans speedily overcame the Russian resistance, did not bother about the Russian forces in their flank and rear and hurriedly proceeded northward.

This unexpected development obliged General von Rennenkampf to withdraw strong forces from his right flank and to reinforce his threatened left wing. Yet this move came too late to prevent the defeat of a Russian division on September 9 near Possessern. But on the next day the Russian left flank had been reinforced by four infantry and three cavalry divisions. The Germans had not yet launched a really serious attack on any of the Russian positions. The Russian general had therefore no reason prematurely to break battle. Nevertheless, he preferred to extricate his troops from the threatening envelopment. During the afternoon of September 9 he ordered the retreat of all Russian units north of the lakes. This order came as a surprise to the Russian troops in the first lines as well as to the Germans who just prepared their main effort. The Russian retreat began in the night of September 10 and was completed without incident.

The Germans had thus won a victory. They had been victorious in an ordinary battle, but they had not achieved a decisive success. The result did not correspond to the hopes of the German leaders. The Russians could not be compelled to fight the battle out to the bitter end. They maintained an open line of retreat and withdrew undisturbed, according to their own will.

Numerically speaking, the situation was much more favourable for the Germans than at Tannenberg. The Germans had 184 battalions, 99 squadrons and 1074 guns against 228 Russian battalions, 173 squadrons and 924 guns. Nor did the quality of

Russian leadership prevent the Germans from winning a more decisive victory. The Russian commander saw dangers which actually did not exist and put his reserves behind his right flank which never was in danger. On the other hand, he failed to protect his left wing and was caught by surprise when the Germans began their envelopment manoeuvre. Consequently, the responsibility for the unsatisfactory outcome of the battle does lie on the German side.

According to the German plan, two thirds of the German forces had to deliver a frontal attack on the Russian front; the last third was ordered to outflank the Russian position. If General von Rennenkampf had continued to fight until September 10 the German leaders would have discovered that their enveloping flank was to weak to achieve a quick and definite success. By then they would have met strong Russian reinforcements and in all probability would have been stopped.

RESERVES WERE LACKING

The Germans did not possess enough reserves to maintain the superiority of their flank after the Russians had thrown in their reserves. After all, since numerical superiority was lacking in the Wattle of the Masurian Lakes, it was indispensable to achieve at least relative superiority at the decisive point. The envelopment operation was conceived as the most important part of the German attack. The decisive point, therefore, was on the German right flank. Consequently, according to theory, the bulk of the German forces had to be used on the right flank.

The commanders of the German Eighth Army disregarded Count von Schlieffen's doctrine in many essential points. Schlieffen considered the flank attack as the essential operation and advised that, in case of insufficient numbers, the necessary numerical superiority must be made available for the flank by delivering the frontal attack with minimum strength. But even with very weak numbers, the forces of the centre have to do more than merely immobilize the enemy by long distance artillery lire. "The enemy front," wrote Schlieffen, "must under all conditions be attacked." The postponement of the German frontal attack during the Masurian battle enabled the Russians to move their reserves behind their left flank. One can be sure that General von Rennenkampf would not have dared to risk his reserves had he envisaged a German onslaught against his centre. A German attack against the Russian northern flank would have been particularly helpful, since it would have incited the Russians, who were already confused by the German radio message, to keep at least some of their reserves in the north.

When on the night of September 9-10 General von Rennenkampf began to retreat, the German offensive against the Russian front had not begun. The German flanking move had not yet progressed sufficiently to deprive the enemy of his initiative. The Russians were not yet enveloped, the German flank was still far from advancing perpendicularly against the Russian positions. Annihilation can only result from an attack from two or three fronts. In the battle of the Masurian Lakes the envelopment of only one flank was feasible. The Germans should therefore have pushed the Russians back to another line and forced Rennenkampf to retreat in an unfavourable direction, preferably to the north against the Haff and the lower Memel. But this was not possible before the German flank, comprising the majority of the German forces, had wheeled around Lake Mauer and was progressing northward. The German offensive never matured. When on September 9 the Russian retreat started, the German centre as well as the German flank still faced due east.

None of the many attempts in World War I to inflict a decisive defeat on the enemy by an attack against one single flank was entirely successful. Most of these attempts led to a greater or smaller victory, but none ended with the annihilation of the enemy. The battles of Leuthen and Zorndorf cannot be easily imitated in modern war. The turning marches which Frederick the Great was still able to perform within a few hours in the immediate vicinity of the battlefield, at present take days, if not weeks; moreover, they spread Out over vast expanses of terrain.

Surprise can hardly be achieved under these circumstances. The opponent prematurely recognizes our intentions and prepares appropriate counter-moves. The enemy can either evade the flanking attack or withdraw his endangered flank. He may also extend his front and counter-attack with new forces.

SUCCESSFUL COUNTER-MOVES

In recent wars such counter-moves were frequently and successfully executed; for instance, by the Russians near Lodz and Wilna. Even in wars under more primitive conditions, it proved to be difficult to annihilate the enemy by a double flank attack. In the Abyssinian War, particularly in the second battle in Tembien and in the battle of Schiré, Badoglio tried to annihilate his enemy by a pincer-attack. He could not accomplish his purpose since the Abyssinians slipped away before the Italian forces joined. In the Chinese War, the main Japanese army under the leadership of General Terauchi could not destroy the Chinese by a combined flank and frontal attack in the battle of Paoting which took place in September, 1937. The Chinese realised the Japanese's intention and retreated before they were effectively turned. Some weeks later the battle of Jengding took a similar course.

The experience of the Germans in the battles of Mons and the Masurian Lakes caused the command of the German Ninth Army to begin the frontal attack in the battle of Vloclavek on whole day earlier than the flank attack. In addition, they placed chiefly cavalry forces on their enveloping flank. However these forces proved too weak to accomplish their task. The Russian leader had enough time to extend his threatened wing and so to forestall any envelopment. Besides, the supporting strong infantry forces, despite a forced march, did not reach the battlefield in time to defeat the Russian forces which successfully held up the German cavalry. The Russians had enough time to retreat, because the Germans were unable to advance deeply into the enemy's flank. All the battles mentioned above show that an enveloping force can never arrive in time if it is organised in deep echelons.

Echelon formations with the main forces in the second line are good only for defence, for it is very difficult to transform them quickly into a formation with the strongest forces in the first line, that is to say, into an offensive echelon. Flanking attacks with defensive echelon formations were rarely successful In recent wars, despite the fact that they sometimes mislead the enemy.

The method of outflanking the enemy with troops taken from the first centre lines, which the Germans tried before Vilna, is still more unsatisfactory. On September 8, 1915, on the eve of the battle of Vilna, seven German divisions (four of which had little value) stood against fifteen Russian divisions south of the river Vilia. North of the Vilia eight and one-half Russian divisions were confronted by ten and one-half German infantry and four cavalry divisions.

The German offensive against Vilna was planned as a decisive operation which should lead to the annihilation of the Russian units. Obviously, the relation of force did not favour such an ambitious undertaking. Already on the first day of battle, September 9, the German northern flank was being immobilised by strong Russian resistance. Only three infantry divisions and one cavalry unit could be made available for the attack on the flank. The German commanders intended to reinforce their attacking flank gradually by units no longer needed on the central front. But superiority on the flank could not be achieved by this method. It is true that the Russians were surprised by the speed of the German wing, but its numerical weakness enabled the Russians to deprive the German flank attack of its strategic, potentialities.

OVERLAPPING OF FRONTS

Instead of letting the encirclement proceed the Russians retreated. At the same time they dispatched strong forces from their central front to the threatened wing. Having all transport facilities of their own country at their disposal, they were quicker than the Germans and, despite almost incredible marching performances of the German troops, extended their line more speedily so that the Russian front soon overlapped the German formations.

Finally, the Russians launched a counter-offensive against the other German flank and on September 26 obliged the German commander, General von Eichhorn, to cease his offensive moves altogether. By this time Eichhorn's forces were confronted by almost double Russian numerical superiority ($18^1/_2$ German infantry and five cavalry divisions against 34 Russian infantry and six cavalry divisions.) The battle of Vilna had taken a course exactly contrary to that planned by the German command.

This battle suggests the conclusion that any attempt to evolve flanking attacks from the first centre lines must prove futile.

An imitation of Frederick's oblique order was never tried in World War I, though this would have been possible by using an echelon formation with its main forces in the first line for the envelopment attack. If an offensive echelon can operate from an angular position against the enemy centre, the chances for decisive victory are much better than if only a defensive echelon is used, as in the battle of Vlocavek. However, such a disposition will not remain secret for long. The enemy will soon find out about the movements of the flank and, since the main forces are in the first line, he will be able to deduce the intended manoeuvre without difficulty. By using offensive echelons, the attacker plays his trump-card first. This is a definite disadvantage which demonstrates the value of the use of offensive echelons for flanking manoeuvres only under exceptional circumstances.

The chances of flank attack would be considerably improved if turning movements could be accomplished more quickly than the advance of the frontally attacking centre. The motorisation of modern armies which permits the setting up of formations with a speed superior to that of the infantry, opens vast new possibilities. The speed of the new land weapons and of the air force has given back to military leadership the chance of surprising the enemy by speed, so that he may be prevented from organizing an appropriate defence in time. An attack from two or three sides against the wings of the enemy has therefore better chances in a future war than during World War I. However, sufficient offensive striking-power of the flanking units, which must at least be strong enough to smash weak and defensive flanks, is still an essential condition for a battle of annihilation. In addition, leadership has to perform the difficult task of coordinating the movements of several units with different speeds and of timing effectively frontal with flank-attacks.

CONCENTRIC MOVEMENTS

A battle of annihilation can also result from concentric movements of independent armies coming from different directions. This strategy led the Prussian Army "from Belle Alliance via Koeniggratz (Sadowa) to Sedan." Theoretically, today it is still the simplest and most promising way to gain a decisive victory. Yet, a concentric operation of the kind requires secrecy. To maintain the secrecy of approaching armies in the era of air power will be more difficult than ever before. In World War I, this strategy was successfully applied at Tannenberg, while in the campaign against Serbia in the autumn of 1915 and during the offensive of the Central Powers against Bucharest at the end of 1916, effective junctions of the independent armies on the battlefield could not be achieved. The encirclement of the Serbian army failed on account of the difficult terrain and the tenacity and skill of the Serbs in defence and retreat. Besides, one of the Austrian flanking armies possessed only insufficient strength while the Bulgarians advanced much too slowly. Nevertheless, the concentric attack pushed the Serbians back into inhospitable regions and put them practically out of the war. In the campaign against Bucharest the Central Powers were hindered by the terrain, the weather and the opponent himself. In particular, the skill and mobility of the Rumanian High Command frustrated the German plan to manoeuvre the Rumanian army into a strategic situation where it could be encircled and destroyed. When the intentions of the Central Powers became clear, the Rumanian commander broke battle and saved his army.

In an operation on outer lines, energetic and unified leadership is indispensable. This has already been pointed out. In both campaigns against the Serbs and the Rumanians, leadership on the side of the Central Powers was much less unified than on the side of their opponents who moreover were lighting on the inner lines. The German and Austrian commanders agreed on the unification of their command only after the decisive battle for Valachia had already begun. Modern technical facilities will certainly help to improve the coordinated command of separate units.

It is no longer necessary, as in the nineteenth century, to issue "directives" in order to regulate the movements of separate units for several days.[3] Operations on outer lines are therefore favoured by technical progress. On the other hand, the technical power of the defence, which is so characteristic for modern war, facilitates operations on inner lines more than concentric attacks. Operations on outer lines are purely offensive enterprises while operations on inner lines are a combination of offence and defence. Considering all elements, a concentric offensive of several armies was more difficult to execute with the weapons of World War I than in the period between Leipzig and Koeniggratz (1815-1866). Schlieffen had foreseen this development and had trained his students for operations on inner lines. Moltke, however, had won his classical victories by operations on outer lines. Since in all modern armies weapons have been introduced to increase the power of offence, the chances of the outer lines have been improved.

The rarity of concentric attacks in World War I must, at least in part, be explained by the fact that the essential conditions for such operations were usually lacking. Shortly after the beginning of the war, the continuous front led to the reemergence of linear strategy. Independent armies were not created and gaps were filled before they even occurred.

SEPARATION AND UNION

Moltke's doctrine that the art of leading big masses consists in having them separated as long as possible and in quickly uniting them on the battlefield soon fell into oblivion. In the autumn of 1914 the art of war fundamentally changed after the battle of the Marne when new methods had to be adopted. The German victories up to this moment were possible because the Germans could impose their law on an enemy entirely taken by surprise. It was clear, however, that the enemy could neither be surprised again on the same front, nor with the same methods. The French had strongly reinforced their left wing and they were careful to prevent new German victories on that flank. Consequently, the Germans could achieve new successes in that sector only if they were able by surprise to concentrate vastly superior masses. Yet the attack by larger forces would have required larger spaces than were at the disposal of the German troops. It would therefore have been necessary to give up a good portion of the conquered territory and to withdraw the whole German army over a considerable distance. Otherwise the necessary space could not be made available. The moral and political consequences of such a bold decision had courageously to be accepted.

It was particularly necessary to prevent the establishment of a continuous front, because flanking attacks are only possible if the front is not continuous. New military units should have been formed and put together in one big shock army. This new army should then have been assembled far behind the front and of course, should have operated independently from the already existing and lighting German units. This is self-evident, according to all military theory. "If one undertakes large scale strategic operations," said Moltke, "the separation of the different armies must be maintained."

The strategic decision which General von Falkenhayn made in the night of September 14-15, 1914, marks a turning point in the history of strategic thought. At first, remaining within the framework of military tradition, he envisaged a continuance of the war of movement and attempts at a new enveloping offensive against the open flank of the Entente. For this, he wished to take the German Sixth Army out of the front in Lorraine and to concentrate it iii the vicinity of Maubeuge, where, as a sort of shock army, it was to operate independent of the rest of the German right wing.

It is doubtful whether this army would have been sufficiently strong for this task. To fill the time-lag between the moment when this decision was made and the moment when the Sixth Army would have been ready to take the field, the right wing of the German army had to retreat in an excentric direction. This was an excellent solution and quite in the spirit of German military tradition. Yet, new strategical ideas determined Falkenhayn's decision. He decided against withdrawing the right wing of the German army and refused to relinquish conquered territory. He was particularly anxious to avoid gaps between his different units, and after some hesitation, dismissed the idea of an excentric retreat. Instead lie resolved to wage a new battle on the Noyon-Reims-Verdun line and to keep the German army as close together as possible.

A CONTRADICTORY TASK

The Sixth Army was transported to the sector of St. Quentin, that is to say, much closer to the German right wing than was originally intended. It was no longer to be used for the offensive exclusively, but also to protect the right wing of the German army. The explanation for this somewhat contradictory task lies in the fact that on September 15, General von Falkenhayn became convinced that Joffre's intentions were similar to his own. The envelopment of the German flank by the French and British could only be avoided by reinforcing the German wing and by extending the front-line.

This was the origin of that singular and fateful operation known to history as the *course à la mer*, the race to the sea. Surprise is, of course, impossible in a race. Both sides know the intentions of the opponent and both sides have the same strategic objective. One is astonished to detect how small a force each of the commanders employed for a battle which both of them considered as decisive and final. Rarely in history were military leaders confronted with a similarly gigantic task and, at the same time, with similarly even chances. But the means both of them employed were insufficient. Joffre and Falkenhayn failed, therefore, by necessity.

The main forces must fight on the front where the decision is sought. If the main attack is to be delivered against the enemy's flank, the main forces must be thrown against it, if possible in a direction perpendicular to that of the central front. There was little chance in September, 1914, to surprise the French by attacks at unexpected times or places. They could only be surprised by superior numbers which should have attacked at a point where a decision was possible. But numerical superiority on the German right flank was impossible without recklessly weakening the centre and the southern flank of the German army.

As a matter of fact, this recklessness was the quintessence of Schlieffen's doctrine. But none of the two commanders dared to concentrate sufficient numbers for the decisive operation, thereby risking the weakening of his other fronts. General Joffre did not find any impressive solution for his strategical problems despite the fact that he was in possession of an excellent railroad system which still was unimpaired. Both commanders committed the same errors and thus prevented a decision on either side. The mistakes of one side were neutralised by the mistakes of the other.

FORCES DRIBBLED AWAY

In the race for the open flank, the method of "too little" prevailed. The forces of both armies were used up in driblets. Despite the bloody sacrifice of the troops, the operation ended in a draw; nowhere a real success was gained. At the end, the original plan to outflank the opponent had evaporated and was replaced by a simple purpose, running faster than the opponent. The race led to the exhaustion of both armies. When it came to a stop, both commanders were confronted with the new and unexpected problem of how to launch frontal infantry attacks against an enemy equipped with modern rifles and machine-guns. An open flank no longer existed.

The *aide de camp* to the German Emperor, General von Plessen, noted on September 28 in his diary: "It is incomprehensible why our right wing cannot defeat the French. Five army corps arc unable to inflict a definite defeat on them, though the French do not have numerical superiority." This remark shows that the problem was not properly understood. Von Plessen ignored that, as a result of the efficiency of modern weapons, defence had become, technically speaking, more powerful than the offensive. Moreover, the difficulties of attack had been considerably increased by the unfortunate strategic dispositions of the German High Command and the complete absence of strategic surprise.

If generalship yields disappointing results, it is habitual to appeal to the morale of [lie troops. In former times, this expedient was sometimes quite successful. In the battles of Leopold of Dessau and Frederick the Great, the Prussian troops, after patriotic appeals, were sometimes capable of taking by a "brutal offensive" even "impregnable positions." In the war of 1870, it was already rather difficult to rely exclusively on heroism and to ignore the deadly effects of modern weapons. Nevertheless, the impressive victory of Gravelotte-St. Privat must largely be ascribed to the valour of the German troops who defeated the enemy despite bad leadership and numerical and technical inferiority. For a long time this "victory put the German army at the top of all European armies" (Count von Schlieffen).

SUCCESS AT HEAVY COST

One should not forget, however, that Gravelotte-St. Prival was one of the bloodiest battles of the nineteenth century, nor that the German success was extremely costly. In modern times, even the utmost bravery is not an efficient expedient against quick-firing artillery and machine guns in prepared positions. German subordinate commanders in 1914, had considerable difficulty in explaining the new situation to their superiors who could not understand why the advance of the troops was so slow in comparison with the speed shown in former wars. If the German leaders had taken into account the incomparable efficiency of modern material, they probably would have understood that appeals to the morale of the troops are futile and that victory is exclusively dependent upon appropriate strategic dispositions, that is to say, upon surprise and concentration of force. Masterly generalship usually has immediate positive effects on the morale of the troops and is much more capable of increasing their courage than even the most impressive and convincing appeals in the order of the day.

On the other hand, unjustified optimism on the part of the High Command has a very negative influence on morale. The troops quickly Jose their confidence if reality substantially differs from the situation as it has been depicted to them by their commanders. Generals who lack the sense for the *realité des choses* tend to wishful thinking, especially in difficult situations.

It must be admitted that during the difficult weeks of 1914, the German High Command and some army commanders indulged in undue optimism. Time and again they were convinced that they had smashed the flank of the enemy and that decisive victory was within their grasp. When a new unit, however small, was thrown into the battle, General von Falkenhayn was confident that it would tip the balance in his favour. He consistently believed that the enemy was exhausted and that his lines were about to crack. Falkenhayn's optimism prevented the German commanders from concentrating a numerically decisive superiority of force on the German right flank.

But the strategy of the French Command in like manner failed. On October 5, 1914, when the battle of Arras had reached its peak, fourteen German divisions fought against fifteen French divisions north of the Somme. That is to say, on the very battlefield where both sides were out to gain a decisive victory, both sides threw approximately only one-sixth of their total strength into this supposedly decisive battle. At that moment, the

German Army had a total strength of 83½ divisions; the Franco-British Army was composed of 85½ divisions. Under such circumstances, definite results cannot be achieved by either side. The only result of this battle was a steady expansion of the front line. Never in history had a similar battle been fought. Commanders of the past would have not understood a battle fought against all the rules of art, developing mechanically and automatically without showing the influence of any strategic idea. Both commanders lacked a creative mind which is so necessary for the solving of new military problems.

On account of technical progress, the art of war had not become inapplicable during World War I. The art of war had not been applied. The principles of concentration at the decisive point and surprise as the means of achieving relative numerical superiority were replaced by the undefinable rules of linear strategy. The war of movement had come to an end.

Instead, a disastrous war of position was fought which could never yield any clear decision.

NOTES

1. Battle of Tannenberg: The Battle of Tannenberg must indeed be considered as a strategic masterpiece. Had the Russians not decisively lost this important battle, they could have continued their offensive into eastern Germany and should have bean able during the first weeks of World War I to advance at least beyond the Vistula. This advance would have fundamentally changed Germanys strategical situation and might have led to an early victory of the Entente.

   At the end of August, 1914, the Russian Army of the Narev moved forward to the west. It was first attacked on its left flank, while its centre continued to advance successfully. When the German attack did not develop satisfactorily, the centre of gravity was shifted against the Russian right wing. Later, the Germans also launched an attack against the rear of the Narev Army. This latter attack was made possible by the previous Russian advance which had driven a wedge into the German lines. The German forces used for the attack on the Russian right wing and rear had been taken out of the front opposite the Russian Army of the Niemen. This army therefore was opposed by practically no German forces.

   The Germans would never have taken the risk of leaving the Niemen Army alone if they had not by their radio monitors learned all important details of the Russian disposition and intentions. If the Russians had attacked with the Army of the Niemen, the Battle of Tannenberg would probably have ended with a German defeat. According to some sources, the inactivity of General von Rennenkampf was due to personal enmity against General Samsonoff.

2. German War Plan: While the German war plan of 1914 against the western powers is usually considered as a strategic masterpiece (despite the fact that driving Great Britain into the war definitely resulted in Germanys defeat) the German war plan in the east was wholly insufficient. The Germans were favoured by luck. Had Russian leadership been more capable, the Germans should have lost the Battle of Tannenberg and would have got into a very difficult situation.

   The main criticism made by the Germans themselves is that they failed to cooperate closely with the Austrian army and to have one single Austro-German war plan against Russia. Both countries together would have been able to oppose the Russian with adequate forces, particularly so if the Austrians had not undertaken the superfluous campaign against Serbia. As it was, each of the countries operated according to its own plan. The consequence of this faulty strategy was that the Austrian army lost its striking power in an unequal offensive light against Russia.

   It is hardly an exaggeration to say that Austria was destroyed during the fall of 1914. It is known that the breakdown of the Austrian empire precipitated the German collapse. Incidentally, it is characteristic of German strategy in 1914 that the Germans had built numerous and strong fortifications in the west, where they intended to fight offensively, but had almost no fortifications in the East, where they planned to remain on the defensive.

3. Speed of Fighting: General Erfurth does not take into consideration that the speed of fighting has considerably increased, in that even with the most perfect communications it will be difficult to receive detailed orders in time. "For every sixty minutes we had at our disposal in muscle-moved warfare, in machine warfare we have nine when faced by tanks and two when faced by aircraft. The old system of command is therefore manifestly useless; for once things get moving there is no longer sufficient time to make out detailed operation orders and filter them down to the troops, the men of action."

   "To do so in a division normally took about eight hours in the last war, and in eight hours a tank may have moved 100 miles or more and an airplane 2,000 . . . In watching and studying (Rommel's) several campaigns it has become clear to me that, so far, he has never worked on what may be called a fixed plan . . . He has relied on rapid decisions, spontaneously made to fit changing events. Instead of working on detailed orders, it would appear that his subordinate commanders have been taught to elaborate their actions from simple ideas and in accordance with a few simple rules . . . It would appear that the secrets of his tactics are to make fuller use of intelligence than of obedience; to impregnate his soldiers with his ideas and then leave it to the men on the spot to elaborate them" (Major General J.F.C. Fuller).

VI

Pursuit, Retreat, Diversion, Counter-Attack

Before the First World War, pursuit was considered one of the essential elements, if not the most essential element of war. Clausewitz pointed out that victory without pursuit never yields great results. Schlieffen, too, thought highly of an energetic pursuit which he regarded as the necessary complement of a battle of annihilation. Pursuit must be undertaken, he taught, irrespective of the fatigue of the troops. No attention should be paid to commanding officers who, on account of the exhaustion of their soldiers, would like to discontinue pursuit.

Nevertheless, "a direct pursuit, however energetically it may be carried out, offers little chance of success." The pursuing infantry as a rule is unable to, march quicker than the retreating enemy. The opponent cannot be forced to accept battle anew, consequently his annihilation cannot be completed. Any pursuit must stop after a short while. Direct pursuit should only be undertaken by weak forces in an effort to win all successes they can without spending themselves in excessive efforts. But the bulk of the pursuing army must not advance in the same direction as the fleeing enemy; instead there should be attempt to cut the enemy line of retreat. Such a pursuit against the enemy's communication line is indispensable if the battle is to end decisively.

The theories of pursuit which date from the time before World War I can be supported by many examples from Napoleon's campaigns, but by not a single example from the wars in the second half of the nineteenth Century. No pursuit occurred in the war of 1866, disregarding one insignificant exception. In the war of 1870-1871, the Prussian army was equally unable to pursue the fleeing enemy, at least not in a manner that would have corresponded to theoretical exigencies. Moltke explained this by his subordinate commanders' lack of understanding of the importance of pursuit.

But other reasons may have been more effective. The most efficient form of pursuit is a march almost parallel to the enemy's line of retreat, aiming at an important objective in the rear of the retreating army. But such a march is possible only under exceptional conditions. On the whole, it is only possible if a strong and early attack has been launched against the enemy's flank and rear. Where the battle consists of frontal operations only, a pursuit to overtake the enemy should not be undertaken.

After a frontal battle, pursuit consists of nothing more than a mere following of the beaten enemy by the victor; both victor and vanquished have to take the same road. This kind of pursuit occurred frequently during the fifty years previous to World War I. In the period of linear strategy, the "frontal pursuit" became the rule. Recent wars re-emphasised the old experience that in a pursuit in which the enemy is merely followed, instead of being cut off from his line of retreat, the vanquished army is soon able to outrun its pursuer, to complete its retreat undisturbed and even to resume battle whenever it choses and its commanders think it is in a position to do so. In the years following the 1914-18 war, however, several classical pursuits were accomplished in minor wars. In August, 1922, the Turks were able to annihilate the Greek army by an effective pursuit which cut the Greek line of retreat. Similarly, the Abyssinians were annihilated while retreating after the battle of Lake Ashangi.

PURSUIT DIFFICULTIES INCREASED

The strong defensive power of modern armament is a new element which further increases the difficulties of pursuit. Generally speaking, most pursuits stop after dusk, or are halted at the next more or less strong natural position defended by a few rearguards. If a pursuit is interrupted once, it is extremely difficult to resume it. Modern technique has not only weakened the attack, but also paralysed pursuit while it favours the possibility of retreat. It may be said that by the development of modern matériel, the whole strategy of retreat has been fundamentally changed. This statement, however, loses its value if the pursuer possesses mastery of the air and large superiority in mechanised and motorised equipment as well. The pursuit operations in the Abyssinian War were exceptionally effective because the Italians could attack the helpless Abyssinians from the air. After the battle in Schiré, the flight of the Abyssinians before the Italian planes assumed "a tragic character." The Abyssinian retreat after the battle of Lake Aschangi became disorderly, not only on account of a successful Italian flanking manoeuvre, but chiefly because of the incessant air attacks.[1]

Before World War I military theory strongly opposed any form of retreat, without even distinguishing between, voluntary retreat and a retreat due to, or forced by, enemy superiority. Even the breaking off of minor engagements was considered a risk. According to the official German doctrine, a unit which with its major forces had been involved in a fight could only under rare circumstances dare a discontinuance of the struggle. Unless the disengaging maneuver was protected by terrain or by strong cavalry, it was said to involve great dangers. Movements to the rear were supposed to be morally disintegrating even if ordered without previous enemy pressure. It was held that voluntary retreat would be equal to an avowal of defeat. Prewar manuals therefore advised that any fight should be continued up to its final decision and, if necessary, by throwing all available reserves into the struggle. Moltke formulated this doctrine in a rather dogmatic way: "He who waits until the opponent has closed, must fight it out." This opinion was perhaps still justified in Moltkes time; yet the disintegrating effects of retreat were certainly overestimated before World War I.

At any rate, Moltke's doctrine lost validity after the machinegun was introduced into modern warfare. For this weapon enables the retreating army to stop the pursuer with only weak rear guards while getting away with its main forces. An orderly and well conducted retreat must be no means lead to a moral crisis. This has repeatedly been proved during World War I. Nevertheless, the official German doctrine stuck to Moltke's formula and even Schlieffen still considered it as valid. He usually refused to accept from his students any solution of military problems in which voluntary retreats were envisaged, regardless of whether the situation would be improved by the proposed retreat. For Schlieffen any retreat was a defeat.

OFFENSIVE RETREAT PRINCIPLE

This attitude on the part of the German authorities was the main reason why the strategic potentialities of voluntary retreats were not understood. In France, the principle of the *retour offensif* was generally accepted, while German writers emphasised only in rare instances that a combination of retreat with counter-attack could be highly effective. In contrast to German conceptions, French strategy and tactics tended to confuse and deceive the opponent. According to the French, the *retour offensif* is one of the most effective means of deception; an especially appropriate method for achieving surprise. Consequently, the army has to be trained not only for attack, but also for retreat and in particular for the difficult switch from retreat to counter-attack.

The French doctrine of strategic retreat was one of the main reasons why, after the loss of the battle of the frontiers, the French High Command quickly determined "to give up terrain in order to organize a counter-attack farther inland," as General Joffre telegraphed to the French Minister of War. The Germans were entirely mistaken about the character and the purpose of the French retreat. They overestimated the significance of their own Successes and thought that they had already imposed their law on the enemy. The official German attitude with respect to retreats also influenced General von Falkenhayn when, in September; 1914, he rejected the idea of withdrawing the German right flank in order to gain increased strength for a renewed attack and, instead of such mobile strategy resolved to fight on in the positions he occupied at the time.

As long as World War I still remained a war of movement, voluntary retreat and pursuit, diversion and counter-attack played an important role on all theatres of war. Modern weapons seemingly eliminate the war of movement in favour of a war of position. But in reality the war of movement was preserved, at least to a certain extent, in operations of elusion and in retreat-counter-attack combinations which, in some instances, must be considered as a particularly energetic form of the war of movement. This is not an entirely new phenomenon; former wars offer many examples for successful counter-attacks after retreat. Clausewitz compared the retreat of a great leader commanding an experienced army to the exit of a wounded lion. Modern warfare offers good opportunities for retreat-counterattack combinations.

In point of fact, most of the really great battles of our time have actually been waged as a counterattack after a retreat (for instance, the Battle of the Marne, the campaign of Lodz, the Serbian counter-offensive late in 1914, the Battle of Warsaw in August 1920). In all these battles, the factor of surprise assumed an important role. Each of these battles began with the unexpected decision to disentangle an army from a difficult position by voluntary retreat. These retreats, if begun in time and commanded skilfully, usually succeeded—contrary to the expectations of pre-World War I military theory. Even if the enemy had envisaged the possibility of retreat, he was usually surprised when the retreat actually started. And from the very beginning of retreat the retreating party usually improved its situation.

RETREAT CONFUSED RUSSIANS

During the night of August 20-21, 1914, the German Eighth Army retreated from the battlefield of Gumbinnen. The Russians were highly surprised next morning, when they discovered this sudden change. However, the Russian command became confused by that unexpected development and ordered that the offensive should not be resumed before the Russian units had rested, reorganised and received reinforcements.

The German leaders on September 10, 1914, were surprised by the unexpected retreat of the Russian Army of the Niemen. Since they did not grasp the intentions of the Russians, they kept their troops back and waited for a further clarification of the Russian tactics.

The Germans had been surprised by the Anglo-French retreat from the Sambre on the night of August 23-24, 1914. The retreat of the Central Powers from Poland in October, 1914, came as an equal surprise to the Russians. General von Mackensen, on October 17, while still attacking Warsaw, confidentially informed his subordinate commanders that a retreat was imminent. After the thorough destruction of railway, telegraph and telephone facilities, the blowing up of bridges and the evacuation of all other military equipment the retreat commenced on the night of October 20. General von Mackensen vanished like a ghost and left nothing behind. Only a few stragglers remained.

The retreat of the Austrian First Army of October 26 on the next day was discovered by the Russians. It was similar to the retreat of the German Eighth Army from the Lötzen-Angerapp position, after the Germans had delivered a successful blow near Stallupoenen on November 7 and 8, 1914. Similarly, the Germans learned about the Russian retreat from Lodz, which began in the evening of December 5, 1914, during the following morning.

The German retreat from the Marne on September 9, 1914,

was a complete surprise for the French High Command. General Joffre did not understand the new situation until a whole day had elapsed. On the evening of September 10 he issued a general instruction in which, for the first time, he informed the French Army of the German retreat and directed an energetic pursuit from the French centre and left flank.

Voluntary elusion and evasion from the enemy is, however, merely the first step towards a greater success. Disengaging from the enemy may bring about a certain easing of a difficult situation. Yet the gain of time which results from voluntary retreats may be partly cancelled by loss of terrain and thereby of space which is necessary for maneuver. Retreat can alter a military situation only if it is used for re-grouping one's forces and for launching a new attack in the right direction. The counter-attack should provide a second opportunity to surprise the enemy (the first surprise having been the timely disentangling from the enemy). This surprise should be accomplished with due regard to time and terrain as well as to the numbers which are required for making the counter-blow sufficiently powerful.

Military writers of pre-World War I times usually recommended retreat in an excentric direction. An excentric retreat was supposed to screen one's own intentions better than a simple retreat along the axis of the previous advance. Moreover, the excentric retreat was believed to render pursuit more difficult. Yet, during World War I, the simple retreat expedient everywhere enjoyed marked preference. One usually withdrew on a broad front, without the idea of launching a new offensive from a rear-position. The intention was merely to continue with a passive defence farther back. The essential factors of strategy—maneuver and movement—were discounted by the tactical conceptions of trench-warfare.

RETREATS IN DEPTH

The deep retreats of the Russian Army in 115 were simple backward movements to new positions. Danilov, the Russian general, rightly considered the absence of manoeuvring as the chief reason why the Russian retreats were so exceptionally deep. Linear strategy, however, reached its peak in the Russian-Polish War of 1920. After the Russian offensive in July north of the Pribjat, the Polish army without offering resistance fell back first on the old German positions from the World War, then with increasing speed to the line Szczata-Niemen, later to the line Bug-Narev and finally almost to the Vistula. This enormous retreat of nearly four hundred miles brought the Polish capital and the battlefield closely together. Marshal Pilsudski blamed the far-reaching results of the Russian victory on the Auta to the trench warfare tactics dear to the heart of the commander of the Polish northern front. Indeed, this officer did not act in accordance with Schlieffen's precept that in order to surprise the enemy one should never take up fixed positions, but must keep moving. He was satisfied with falling back from one fortified line to the other, instead of trying to stop the Russian offensive (as Pilsudski had recommended) by maneuver and counter-attack.

Tuchatchevski, the Russian commander-in-chief admitted that after the Russian victory of July 4, 1920, he had no clear ideas about the intentions of the Poles. It was therefore difficult for him to take appropriate measures. After any success, he wrote some years later, the commander of the victorious army is confronted by a difficult choice. Shall he continue his offensive in the former general direction and maintain the existing disposition of his forces, or shall he re-group and select another direction? Shall he leave all his forces in the front-line or shall he form a reserve force? Shall he, therefore, pursue with weak forces and have strong reserves ready in case the reinforced enemy strikes back or shall he recklessly advance? Tuchatchevski rightly emphasised that an army can hardly be re-grouped during a speedy offensive, particularly if the destruction of railway facilities makes the shifting of large units almost impossible.

These were the same difficulties which in August, 1914, confronted the German chief-of-staff after the Franco-British army

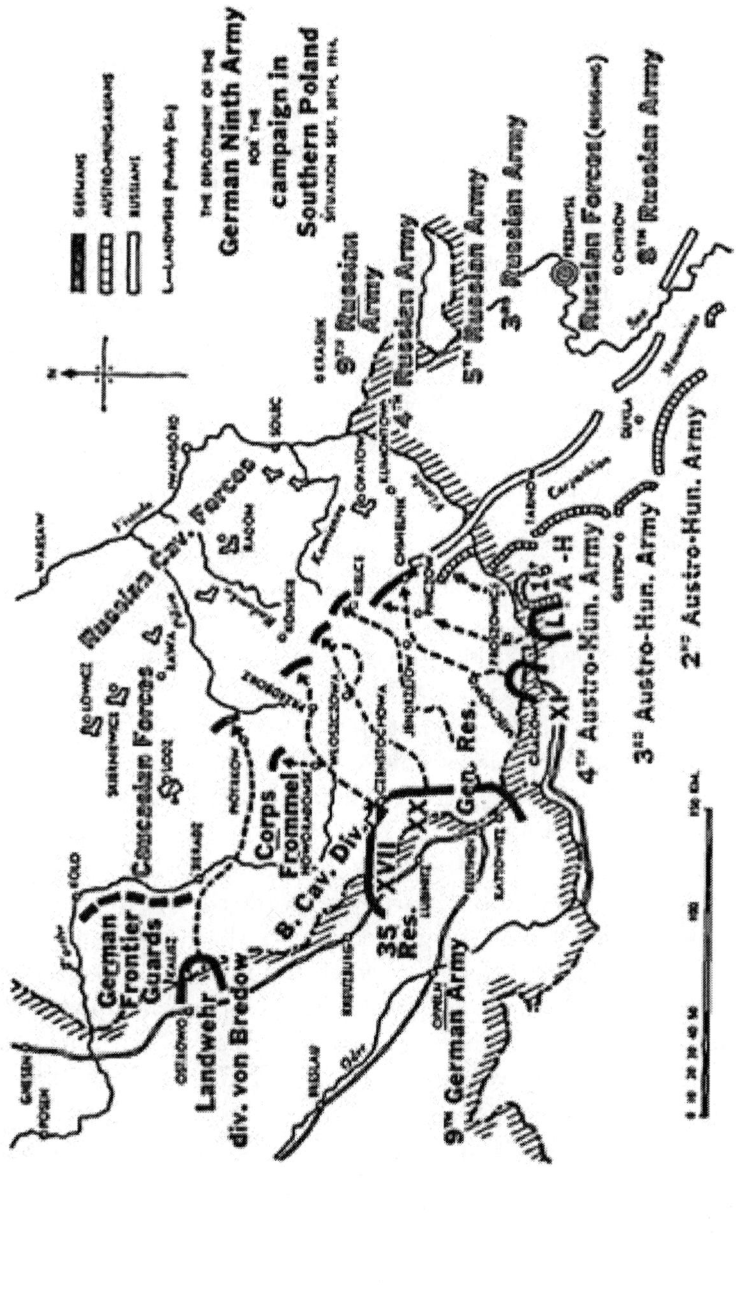
The deployment of the
German Ninth Army
for the
campaign in
Southern Poland
Germans
Austro-Hungarians
Russians
Russian Cav. Forces
Caucasian Forces
German Frontier Guards
Landwehr
div. von Bredow
Corps Frommel
8. Cav. Div.
35 Res.
XVII
XX
Gd. Res.
9TH German Army
4TH Austro-Hun. Army
3RD Austro-Hun. Army
2ND Austro-Hun. Army
9TH Russian Army
4TH Russian Army
5TH Russian Army
3RD Russian Army
Russian Forces
8TH Russian Army

had begun to fall back on the Marne. Actually, the Russians did not expect that the Poles would still be able to execute strategic maneuver. They counted upon a simple retreat on a broad front which, at the beginning, the Poles carried out. The Russians hoped to disintegrate the Polish army by merely pursuing them. Neither side ever thought of surprise operations, though the possibilities for very effective surprises were certainly not lacking for either army. In particular, the Poles would have been able to lay a trap for the Russians. The retreating army is usually better informed about the opponent and what he is doing than the pursuer, especially in the former's own country. During the advance to the Marne, the German Army could learn many details about the advantages of lighting in their own country.

DOUBTS AND POSSIBILITIES

Military writers sometimes tend to doubt the possibility of strategic surprise. They allege that surprise can never be achieved, unless the opponent has previously been forced to occupy those very positions which the surprising party wants him to occupy. Otherwise the opponent could never be out-manoeuvred and surprise accomplished. The opponent must either be immobilised or else completely unable to move and to maneuver. It is inserted that unless he passively permits himself to be enveloped, surprise is out of the question.

These doubts seem to be partly justified, yet history shows that not only surprises have effectively been staged, but that also the attacked army usually contributed its own share to the success of the attacker. Nevertheless, the switch from retreat to attack is an extremely complicated maneuver and is dependent upon some kind of aid from the pursuer. According to Schlieffen, the main difficulty is to deprive the enemy of his initiative and to regain the initiative for oneself after it had been lost in previous phases of the battle. To remain on the defensive and to continue with a retreat until the favourable moment arrives, requires strong nerves and Napoleon's *coup d'oeil* for strategic possibilities. The decision must be made at a moment when possibilities can only be dimly discerned.

The difficulties which oppose the strategy of counter-offensive revealed themselves clearly during the operations of August, 1914, in Alsace-Lorraine. During these operations, the opinions, orders and counter-orders of the highest German military authorities did not cease wavering.[2] Count von Schlieffen was certainly justified in saying that lack of harmony between the intentions of the commander-in-chief and the independence and initiative of subordinate commanders constitutes the main trouble of big armies. Harmony may only be achieved, says Schlieffen, if the commanders of the different army groups adapt themselves to the ideas of the commander-in-chief, so that only one single thought directs the entire army.

In Alsace-Lorraine, the divergence of views had to be eliminated by a clear order from the High Command. But on both German flanks, the necessary energy of command was lacking. Instead of issuing clear and binding orders, the High Command contented itself with "wishes" and "proposals" and timidly gave in when the subordinate did not deign to accommodate himself to the desires of the chief.

TRAPS AND THEIR CHANCES

Military theorists are fond of asserting that successful surprises are more or less improbable because the enemy rarely runs into a trap which has been set for him. This prejudice was the main reason why at the outbreak of World War I in 1914, the commander of the German Sixth Army gave up the promising plan of falling back behind the river Saar and withdrawing on the Lorraine front in order to lure the French into Germany and to attack them at both flanks after they had driven a sufficiently deep wedge into the German lines. True, Marshal Joffre after the war affirmed that he would not have marched into a sack which the Germans had obligingly opened for him. This statement, however, does not prove that he would not actually have helped

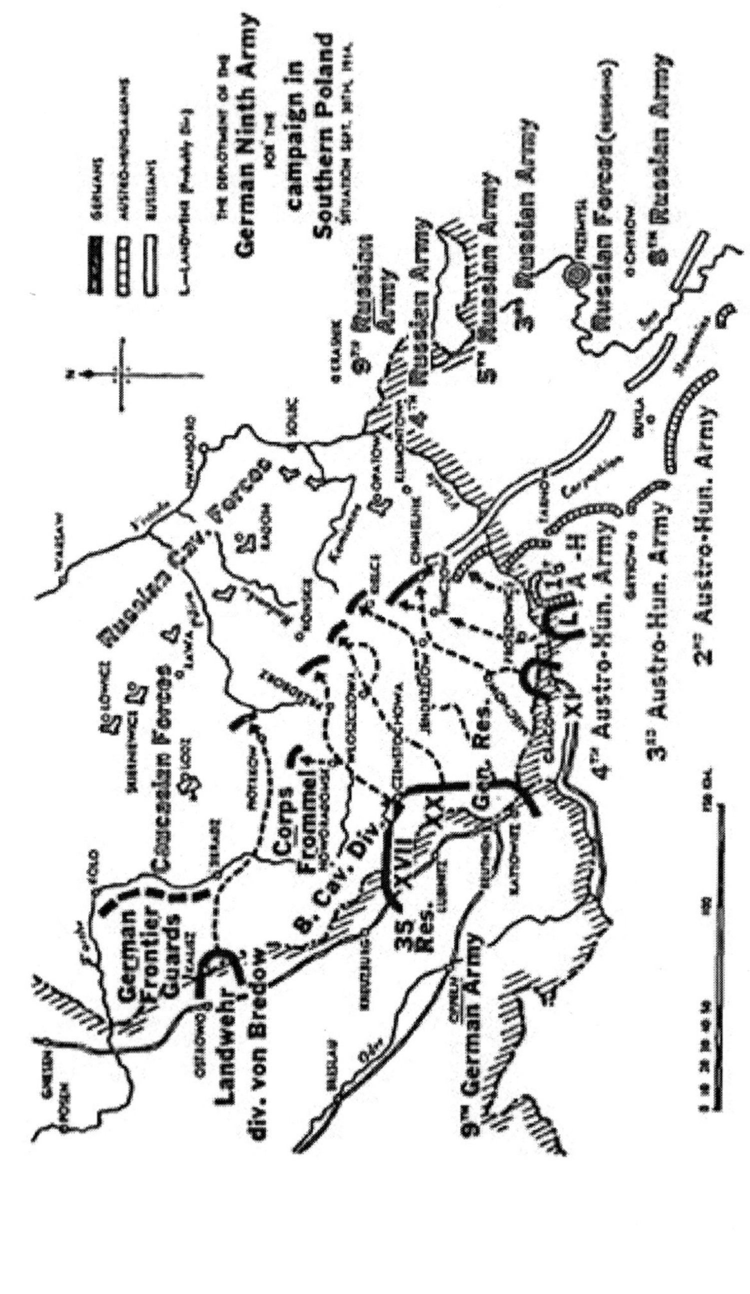
German Ninth Army
campaign in Southern Poland
Russian Cav. Forces
Caucasian Forces
German Frontier Guards
Landwehr
div. von Bredow
Corps Frommel
8. Cav. Div.
35 Res.
XVII
XX
Gd. Res.
XI
9th German Army
9th Russian Army
4th Russian Army
5th Russian Army
3rd Russian Army
Russian Forces
8th Russian Army
4th Austro-Hun. Army
3rd Austro-Hun. Army
2nd Austro-Hun. Army

the Germans by walking into the trap. At any rate, he had given orders to the French First and Second Army to attack in direction of Saarburg. These orders permit us to question whether his post-war assertion has any real historical value.

To choose the right moment for the start of an undertaking of any kind is very difficult. But in strategy the choice of the right moment is particularly hard and, moreover, is of crucial importance. Striking too soon means spoiling even a perfect chance. The commander must not permit himself to be taken in by the enthusiasm of the troops. He should not follow their natural impulse to advance but, if need be, should be able to check his troops and curb forward movements, however promising they may look to victorious soldiers.

The German Army began the Battle of Lorraine too soon, hence it could win only an "ordinary victory." The French did not expect a German counter-attack on August 20, and were effectively caught by surprise. But the German counter-attacking forces were too weak and the direction of the German move did not correspond to the strategic plan. It proved to be impossible to force the enemy into a different position. The French were attacked only frontally. Therefore, they were able to disengage and to withdraw to their original positions. The German attempt at least to cut the retreat of some French units was unsuccessful, in spite of the fact that the German units were ordered to pursue relentlessly in the direction of the Meurthe.

A counter-attack by an army retreating on a broad front is not easy. It is particularly difficult to choose a direction that may yield strategic results. Frequently, the counter-attacking units will crash head-on into a strong enemy line. It is also possible that two attacks clash and that no result will be achieved despite a bloody and exhausting fight.

RESULTS AT ST. QUENTIN

This, for instance, was the fate of the counter-attack of the French Fifth Army near St. Quentin on August 29-30, 1914, the failure of which was easily predictable. It may be presumed that General Joffre intended at first merely a diversion-attack to relieve the hard-pressed British army. However, General Lanrezac objected to this project with apparently rather good reason and the French generalissimo had to use strong language to make himself obeyed. He declared that the fate of the whole campaign depended upon Lanrezac's attack on St. Quentin and that, by means of surprise, this move could give "decisive results." He asked General Lanrezac to execute his orders "*sans discuter.*"

Lanrezac was not convinced, but began the attack in the morning of August 29. The course of events proved him to be right and disproved General Joffre. It is true that the French counter-attack was a complete surprise for the German command and for most of the German divisions. On the western bank of the Oise, a serious crisis occurred in German ranks. However, the situation was soon well in hand again and the French did not succeed in forcing the Germans on the defensive. On the second day, the attack of the French Army petered out and the Germans launched an attack of their own from the southern bank of the Oise near Guise.

Some hours later, the French Fifth Army was already in difficulties; General Lanrezac reported to the commander-in-chief that his army might be cut off, if it remained much longer in the present position. Since he was under formal and strict orders to attack he would Continue to do so, but not on his own responsibility. Instead, the French High Command itself had to assume the responsibility for this operation. General Joffre was not prepared to accept such a heavy risk. During the night of August 29-30, he ordered the French Fifth Army to resume its retreat. General Lanrezac received this order late in the morning of August 30, and was obliged to break off battle in plain daylight. During the disengagement, the French suffered heavy losses and could retreat but slowly.

As a consequence of this two-day-battle and the subsequent retreat, the French Fifth Army had lost much of its striking power.

Yet the Germans let the French go and most of the German soldiers were permitted to rest. The German commanders were content with pursuing the French with artillery and smaller infantry detachments in light marching order. Such a pursuit, of course, could not lead to any real success. One may be sure that under similar circumstances Count von Schlieffen would have driven ahead and paid not the least attention to the fatigue of the troops and the apprehensions of the commanding generals.

Incidentally, the conduct of the Battle of St. Quentin was greatly facilitated for the Germans by the seizure of important documents. On the evening of August 29 they captured the chief-of-staff of one of the French corps who carried the complete French order of attack in his pocket. This order revealed every detail of the. French plan and informed the Germans of the numerical strength of the French. The information proved to be very helpful on the second day of the battle.

RESULT IN EAST PRUSSIA

In East Prussia the Germans were more successful with a combined retreat-counter-attack than the French near St. Quentin. On November 6, 1914, they stopped their retreat beyond the Prussian eastern frontier. On November 7, 1914, they launched a counter-attack against the Russian forces in the vicinity of Stallupoenen. Because the region of Lake Wysztyt and the brushwoods of Rominten can hardly be negotiated by strong formations, the commander of the German Eighth Army had correctly foreseen that the Russians would divide their forces into two parts. This was a good opportunity to attack the Russian units which passed north of this impenetrable sector, namely the Russian Third Corps. This corps could be attacked from the region of Stallupoenen on both flanks by a corps under General von Bulow and in addition by the German First Corps which proceeded by forced marches into the vicinity of Tollmingkehmen. On November 7, the Germans attacked the advancing Russian Third Corps (which had just been reinforced) on both sides of the Wirballen-Stallupoenen railroad and also the Russian Cavalry corps near Mehlkehmen under General Gurko which protected the Russian left flank. The Russians were hard hit by this surprise attack and alter having suffered heavy losses retreated beyond the German frontier. The engagement of Stallupoenen may serve as an example for a well planned and executed diversion attack. Despite numerical inferiority, the Germans were able to concentrate superior numbers in the region where they intended to strike. Their surprise attack was therefore successful.

The Austrian offensive in December, 1914, which was aimed at the southern wing of the Russian army under the command of General Dimitriev and which led to the battle of Limanova-Lapanov shows strategical similarities. It also ended with a marked success. According to the testimony of General Russki, who at that time commanded the Russian northwestern front "this dashing operation completely surprised the Russians and hit them at the most vulnerable spot of their entire front." General Russki rightly called the battle of Limanowa "a strategical masterpiece."

REASONS FOR RESULTS

On the whole, a strategic counter-attack after a preceding retreat is a more ambitious, and hence more difficult, enterprise than a diversion-attack with limited objectives. In recent wars, a *retour offensif* has been sometimes attempted in order to alter the strategic situation as a whole. We shall now discuss some of these attempts and see why they have or have not been successful. In particular, we shall try to determine what role the factor of surprise played during these operations.

The analysis of the Battle of the Marne in September, 1914, yields interesting results. First, it shows that the French made their counter-attack with astonishingly weak forces which were certainly not in proportion to their task; and, secondly, that the Germans really had been surprised by the French maneuver.

The French generalissimo was not alone responsible for the assembly of a new army in the region of Paris: This measure must in part be attributed to the French Minister of War, Messimy, who claims to have been solely responsible for it. However this may be, Messimy asked on August 25 that three French corps should be earmarked for the defence of Paris. The next day, the Governor of Paris, General Galliéni, who worried about the security of the French capital, insisted on the urgent dispatch of additional troops to Paris. Had these troops not been formed into the Army of Paris, the French attack on the right German wing would have been still weaker than it actually was. As it was, the old principle that one must be strongest at the decisive point was by, no means adhered to.

At the end of the five-day battle on the Ourcq, the German First Army comprised 128 battalions. These German battalions were attacked by 127 French battalions, and at the beginning of the battle even by a lesser number. It is true that the French fought in conjunction with 64 British battalions, yet at the most decisive point of this battle, at the extreme left wing of the French army, the Germans possessed almost threefold superiority.

The German command had thus accepted the risk of being numerically weaker on most parts of the front in order to concentrate a real striking power at the focal point. If the French desired to win a final victory on the Marne, they should have attacked with overwhelming odds. In discussing a similar strategic situation, Schlieffen once remarked that a flanking attack against the enemy's line of retreat should never be launched "with four corps, but with everything one has."[3] With a superiority of a few divisions the French could not expect to disrupt the German front, let alone overthrow the German army. It is true that the French commander did not have so ambitious a plan. He did not wage a decisive battle north of Paris; he merely attempted a limited counter-attack against the two German flanks on the Meuse and near Paris respectively, without-forming a centre of gravity on either spot.

GALLIÉNI VS. JOFFRE

General Galliéni had a much clearer view of the German situation, but Joffre was not at all pleased with the former's proposal to attack strongly the flank of the German First Army. At first, Joffre even refused to be dragged into a "premature offensive." Galliéni, however, accepted no refusal and insisted that the circumstances were favourable for a counter-attack, since the flank of the German Army was protected by only one single corps. Joffre finally realised the opportunity himself and on September 4 accepted the Plan of his subordinate.

The Germans made many contributions of their own to the success of the French counter-attack. After the battle of the frontiers, the German High Command believed the French to be in full retreat towards Paris. They expected the French to make several stands, first behind the Aisne and then behind the Marne. They also considered possible a French concentration on the lower Seine and believed in a French diversion-offensive in Lorraine. The German Army was therefore ordered to pursue the French to Paris. The German High Command evidently exaggerated the importance of the victories which had already been won. The French were supposed to be exhausted and a *retour offensif* was considered out of question.

According to the German High Command, relentless pursuit would definitely break down French resistance. Consequently, no re-grouping of the German forces nor a concentration of strong forces at one point was deemed to be necessary. On the evening of August 30 the German High Command changed the direction of the advance and turned the wing of the German army from southwest to south. On September 2 the German High Command announced its intention to push the French back to the southeast, instead of forcing them into Paris. The German First Army was ordered to advance more slowly than the Second Army whose flanks it had to cover.

At that moment, however, the German chief-of-staff received advance warning of impending misfortune. Air reconnaissance disclosed that the French had begun to move large bodies of troops to the southwest. In spite of the hot German pursuit, the French, with the help of their railways, were apparently still capable of re-grouping. On the next day, these reports were confirmed and the Germans suspected that the French withdrew troops from Lorraine, a conjecturer which was confirmed on the afternoon of September 4. The German commander could no longer doubt that the French were preparing a large scale counter-blow.

On the same day serious trouble arose for the German chief-of-staff. He suddenly received unexpected information that the German First Army, instead of following the German Second Army farther behind, had crossed the Marne west of Chateau-Thierry. In the evening of September 4 he had a radio message from the First Army informing him that this army had continued its advance during the whole day. The First Army tried to envelop the French Army in a southeastern direction, while the protection of its flanks had been entrusted to small forces.

ATTACK FROM PARIS FEARED

What would happen if the French launched a strong attack from Paris? Was there still a chance to forestall the danger which menaced the German right flank? The moment had come to reconsider whether the operations just in execution were to be continued, or if the maintenance of the original plan would not lead into serious trouble. Had the German operation still a good chance to warrant tie acceptance of heavy risks? The German chief-of-staff was confronted by the alternative of either stopping the pursuit of the French army and re-grouping his forces for a new operation, or of leaving everything as it was and continuing the advance. He adopted the latter solution and thus contributed to the success of the French counter-attack.

The French enterprise was also being favoured by unexpected luck and favourable circumstances. Still, as late as the evening of September 4 it was possible to protect effectively the German right wing against a French blow from Paris. It was merely necessary to re-group the German First Army. The German commander-in-chief issued an order to that purpose, but unfortunately worded it in so complicated a way that it was not understood by his subordinates. The order ran as follows: "First and Second Army remain in front east of Paris, the First Army between Oise and Marne, the Second between Marne and Seine."

When Moltke wrote this order he already knew that a great part of the First Army stood south of the Marne and had advanced far away from the Oise. Instead of ordering the First Army to remain east of Paris, he should have ordered the retreat to the positions between Oise and Marne. This retreat was unavoidable, if the German flank was to be protected at all. Besides, the commander of the First Army should have been informed about the re-grouping of the French army, but for some reason or other he never received this vital information.

AIR SURVEY INCOMPLETE

To make things even worse, the First Army completely failed to reconnoiter in direction of Paris. The available aircraft was used only for reconnaissance to the south. The Second Army reconnoitered in the same direction; the extreme German flank had no aircraft at all. Only one corps reconnoitered to the west and indeed did not fail to report the concentration of strong French forces northeast of Paris. This report, however, was not transmitted to the commander of the First Army. The lack of information was therefore exclusively due to the faulty use of air reconnaissance.

Yet the commander of the First Army interpreted it as proof that the German flank was safe. Consequently, General von Kluck on September 5 continued his advance to the south, thus getting further away from Paris. A rapid forward movement, he felt, would hasten the disintegration of the French army. Some of his officers warned him, however, of the great risks involved in this advance, yet he rejected their objections as being "imaginations

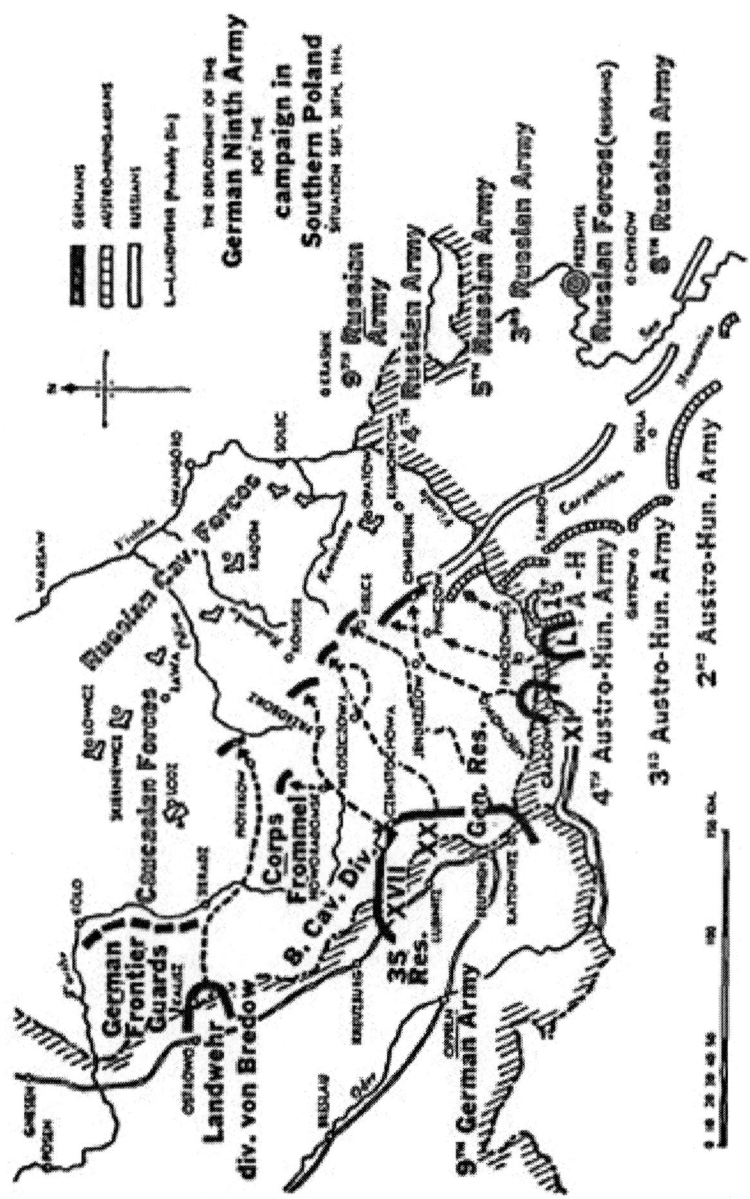
The deployment of the
German Ninth Army
for the
campaign in
Southern Poland
German Frontier Guards
Landwehr
div. von Bredow
9th German Army
35 Res.
B. Cav. Div.
XVII
XX
Gd. Res.
Corps Frommel
Caucasian Forces
Russian Cav. Forces
XI
1st A.-H.
4th Austro-Hun. Army
3rd Austro-Hun. Army
2nd Austro-Hun. Army
9th Russian Army
4th Russian Army
5th Russian Army
3rd Russian Army
Russian Forces
8th Russian Army

of pessimistic minds." He saw the situation of the enemy through the lens of his own wishes and refused to be disturbed by the "Ghost of Paris" until he had seen it in flesh and blood.

So the singular situation arose that the governor of Paris was lying in wait for his game and spotted all the movements of the Germans. Galliéni could deliberately choose the right moment, because the Germans had concentrated their attention to the south and ignored the dangers from Paris. They continued to march southward thereby more and more uncovering their flank, against which a lurking enemy was about to strike a hard blow.

As it was, the French attack on September 5 from. Paris took the German First Army completely by surprise. On that day, the disposition of the German units was particularly unfavourable. The danger for the whole German flank was extreme. The numerical weakness of the French attacking forces was solely responsible for the limited French success, although the German leaders at last became equal to their responsibilities and, together with their troops, showed themselves able to master a particularly difficult situation. Had the French attacked with stronger forces, a disaster for the German army would have been unavoidable. Had the French attacked with double or triple the strength of Galliénis force, and had they encountered an opponent of lesser military qualities, their attack would possibly have decided the whole war.

In the Battle of the Marne, the French commander certainly sinned against the principle of concentration. His mistake was repeated by the German chief-of-staff when in November, 1914, he sought not only to smash by a counter-attack the right flank of the Russian army, but by pressing against their rear to force the Russians to accept battle on a reversed front. If General von Falkenhayn with twelve German corps had adhered to his original plan of making a surprise attack in the region of Thorn, a great victory would have been won aid the war in the east would perhaps have been triumphantly ended.

VICTORIES BRED CRISIS

The German Eastern Army was to weak for such an ambitious undertaking. Big victories require big means. The offensive of Lodz, attempted with insufficient forces, came quickly to a standstill and despite brilliant victories led to a serious crisis for the Germans. It miscarried because it proved to be impossible to maintain numerical superiority throughout the battle.

The Germans started their offensive under particularly favourable circumstances. The German commander knew all the details of the Russian strength, disposition anti organisation. In the last minute, he learned beyond any doubt that the Russians had ceased to advance farther to the south. Hence he was able to take strong forces away from the southern front and to organize an offensive centre of gravity in the area of Thorn. The reports of German air reconnaissance and of the German land forces were confirmed by lengthy Russian radio messages which the Germans deciphered without difficulty. Thus, the enemy facilitated the German preparations for a battle of annihilation. It was only necessary to hide from the Russians the transport of German shock-troops from southern Poland and East Prussia to Thorn. Extensive precautions were taken to keep the German troop movements secret. *The weaker one's own force, the more is surprise essential.*

The successful surprise of the Russians was facilitated by a set of favourable conditions. The Russians did not yet possess modern air reconnaissance. The brevity and relative darkness of November days made the screening of marches and railway transports comparatively simple. The concentration of the German offensive force could be covered by German cavalry because the Russians remained passive and were not at all eager to learn about developments behind the German lines. The Russians ignored the fact that some German formations had been diverted from southern Poland to another front; the Russian cavalry had failed to push on with its pursuit behind the retreating German Eighth Army. There is little doubt, therefore, that the Germans were favoured by luck when preparing the maneuver of Lodz.

If motorised reconnaissance units had existed at that time, heavy railroad traffic almost under the noses of the Russians could hardly have remained unnoticed. Besides, the speed of the German maneuver contributed to the success of the surprise operation. The decision to attack the northern Russian flank was made on November 3. On November 4, the assembly of the German attack formation began. On November 10, the German concentration was terminated and the German cavalry began its forward movement. On November 11, the offensive started in full.

The Russians unwittingly and, carelessly continued to inform the Germans about their dispositions by transmitting inter-army orders and intelligence in clear by radio. Like General Galliéni before the Battle of the Marne, General vomi Mackensen prior to the offensive of Lodz knew everything about the Russian situation. In addition, the Russians failed to discover the

German concentration near Thorn and learned of the impending storm only a short while before the Germans actually began to move.

FRUITS OF SURPRISE LOST

This surprise concentration of the German Ninth Army was an excellent performance and had been recognised as such by the Russians themselves. General Danilov writes: "Our slowness and incapacity for gaining information of the opponent must be contrasted with the German speed and with their accomplished art of maintaining secrecy. Therefore, their blow caught us entirely by surprise."

Neither German efficiency nor the luck by which the Germans were favoured, nor finally the information which unconsciously the Russians vouchsafed to the Germans were, however, sufficient for gaining a really decisive success. The surprise which had so brilliantly been accomplished was not exploited by the Germans who failed to achieve numerical superiority at the decisive point. They did not succeed in concentrating more troops than the enemy expected. Obviously, surprise alone can never be effective, it is only a *condition* of success, not the success itself. *Surprise must be supplemented by numerical superiority which, under all conditions, remains the most important objective of the strategical art and the most general principle of victory.* (Clausewitz).

The offensive of Lodz, it is true, was begun on the German side with a small margin of superiority, but this margin was speedily lost. Eleven German infantry and five cavalry divisions marched on November 11 against four Russian infantry and five cavalry divisions. Up to November 25, when the offensive finally stopped, the Germans had been reinforced by five weak Landsturm brigades, that is to say, by a second-rate reserve force, hardly suitable for active warfare. During the same period, Russian infantry had grown to 26½ divisions. Altogether about 123 German battalions with about 800 guns fought against 204 Russian battalions with 750 guns in the region of Lodz. In the area of Lovitch, the situation was still more unfavourable for the Germans. Here, 34 German battalions with 100 guns were opposed by 160 Russian battalions and 384 guns.

In a modern battle, even the highest heroism cannot compensate for such inferiority. The overwhelming importance of numerical superiority did not diminish in the least with the improvement of modern materiel, regardless of whether it is absolute or merely a relative superiority achieved by good generalship. The failure to concentrate sufficient forces for the Lodz offensive was largely due to the fact that Germany had to wage war on two separate fronts.

Before World War I, Count von Schileffen had often discussed the strategic implications of a simultaneous war against France and Russia. He repeatedly pondered situations which necessitated the shifting of the main effort from one front to the other. Schlieffen emphatically warned against dividing the German Army so that it would be numerically weaker on both fronts. According to him, the minimum force for large-scale strategic operations against Russia was an army of nine to eleven corps.

To conclude this chapter, we desire to discuss several examples of successful strategic counter-attacks. The Serbian campaign of autumn 1914 is one of the most impressive examples of that kind. The Serbian commander-in-chief, Voyvod Putnik, evaded the Austrian-Hungarian offensive until the Austrian army had over-extended its communication lines and slowed down its movements. The Serbian leader had strong enough nerves to wait for a long time for striking back, though the Serbian army had suffered severely under the strain of the continuous retreat and though the commanders of the Serbian armies urged an early counter-offensive.

CONCENTRATION AND SURPRISE WON

The Serbian counter-offensive was launched after the Serbian wing had been strongly reinforced. The Serbs had concentrated their main striking power at the point where they wished to make their main effort. The Serbian counter-offensive proved to be highly successful, particularly because he Austrian commander, General Potiorek, did not believe that the Serbs were still able to attack. He thought that after long weeks of retreat the Serbs were at he end of their rope. Thus, Putnik held both trump cards, surprise and concentration, in his hands and achieved with his little army a brilliant victory against two entire Austro-Hungarian armies.

The most impressive example of a surprise-counter-attack is the Battle of Warsaw which decided the Russian-Polish war. On the night of August 7-8, 1920, the Polish northern front continued its retreat from the line Biala-Janov, north of Siedlce-Sokolov-Rozan. During the retreat, the Polish army was to be re-grouped for the counter-offensive ordered by Marshal Pusudski on August 6. This offensive was based upon the fundamental idea that the Poles should hold a line along the Orzyclarev rivers and along the Vistula as far down as Ivangorod. They should also try to retain the strongly fortified bridge-heads of Modlin and Warsaw. The main Polish attack was to be launched from the

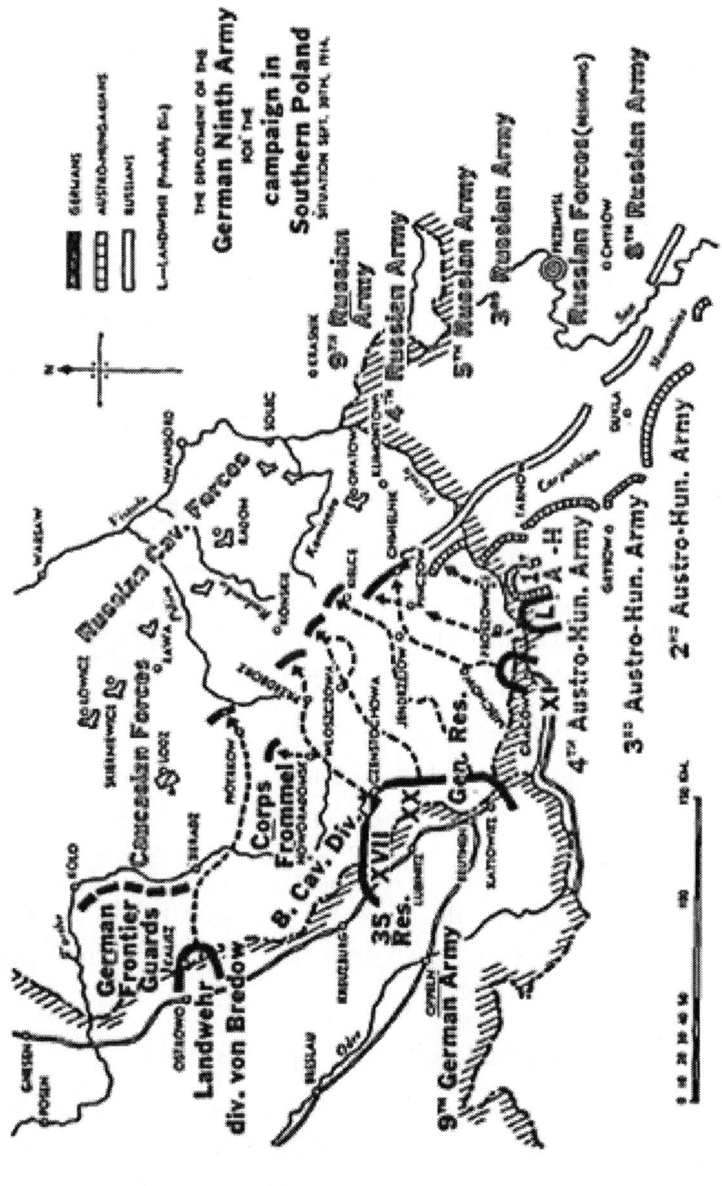
German Ninth Army
campaign in
Southern Poland
9th German Army
Landwehr
div. von Bredow
German Frontier Guards
8. Cav. Div.
35 Res.
XVII
XX
Gd. Res.
Corps Frommel
Caucasian Forces
Russian Cav. Forces
9th Russian Army
4th Russian Army
5th Russian Army
3rd Russian Army
Russian Forces
8th Russian Army
4th Austro-Hun. Army
3rd Austro-Hun. Army
2nd Austro-Hun. Army

positions along the Wieprz river to the north and northeast against the southern flank of the advancing Russians. The Polish striking force was to comprise two infantry divisions and one cavalry brigade of the Polish southern front and three and one-half infantry divisions of the Polish northern front. During the evening of August 7, the Polish Fourteenth, Sixteenth and Twenty-first infantry divisions held positions southwest and west of the Bug river, as it is shown on the map. In the following nights, these divisions retreated due west to the line Siedlce-Lucov-Kock. During the night of August 11-12, they turned around and moved southward to the Wieprz river.

This perpendicular march across the axis of the enemy's advance resembles somewhat, the German deployment for the Battle of Tannenberg. The Russian Army of the Niemen in 1914 ignored the frontal march of two German corps. Similarly in 1920, the Russian Sixteenth Army and the Russian High Command failed to discover the departure of three Polish divisions to the southwest and south. Tuchatchevsky, the commander of the Russian western front made the *a priori* assumption that the Poles would continue to retreat behind the Vistula. He was therefore also convinced that the three Polish divisions which had disappeared were continuing their retreat to the west.

Tuchatchevsky was firmly resolved not to change his opinions concerning his opponents attitude. He had the "strong conviction" that the Poles would never accept a decisive battle east of the Vistula with the river in their rear, but would use the Vistula as a military obstacle. Hence they would concentrate their forces west of the river and so protect their capital and their vital supply line with the port of Dantzig.

POLES SURPRISED RUSSIANS

Tuchatchevsky planned to concentrate his main strength on his northern flank in order to envelop the Polish left wing north of Warsaw. His own left wing had to deliver a frontal attack on the bridgehead of Warsaw. For the protection of the Russian left wing itself, Tuchatchevsky had earmarked only a small force. To protect himself in that zone he counted entirely upon the early arrival of the Russian Twelfth Army and of a large cavalry force which was still held up near Lemberg. His plan, however, was purely wishful thinking, for the expected reinforcements for the Russian left flank failed to appear.

In conclusion, three Russian armies moved northward while the Russian Sixteenth Army operated directly towards Warsaw with its main concentration in the northern sector of battle-field. The protection of the Russian left flank became the mission of the small Mosyr group, some four thousand men, which was ordered to move forward towards Parczev-Ivangorod. This strange disposition of the Russian army certainly facilitated the execution of Marshal Pilsudski's plan. The three Polish divisions which marched southward to take up their positions on the Wieprz disengaged themselves from the enemy and marched along his front without great difficulties. They were only in intermittent contact with the Mosyr group and could calmly prepare for their counter-attack.

Not even once did Tuchatchevsky consider the possibility that Polish units would be diverted from the northern to the southern front. This is the more astonishing, as the Russian High Command for a long time had already expected a Polish counteroffensive from the area of Ivangorod and repeatedly drew Tuthatchevsky's attention to this danger. The Russian commander did not even become doubtful when the southern flank of his Sixteenth Army failed to encounter any Polish resistance.

WHERE WERE THE POLES? HAD THEY RETREATED FROM THIS FRONT?

Tuchatchevsky did not doubt for one moment that the Poles had retreated to the west. When some days before the start of Pilsudski's' offensive an army order was found on a dead Polish officer revealing the concentration of a new Polish army south of Warsaw, Tuchatchevsky considered this as a ruse to mislead him.

Like many other generals, he fancied a situation based on personal wishes, not on reality.

As a consequence of these errors, which occurred despite repeated warnings, the Soviet leaders were fully surprised by the Polish counter-offensive of August 16 against the Russian southern flank from the Wieprz. The success of this strategic *retour offensif* was beyond expectation. The numerical weakness of the Polish offensive-group was more than compensated by the exhaustion of the Russian troops which were tired by forced marches of five weeks. The Poles achieved numerical superiority at their point of attack and inflicted a crushing defeat on the Mosyr group. The Russian Sixteenth Army was unfavourably deployed at the time of the Polish attack and as quickly overrun. The Poles continued their northward advance and attacked the flanks of the Russian Third and Fifteenth Army. These armies tried hard to stop the Polish offensive and to keep open a line of retreat for the Russian Fourth Army which had advanced far to the west. But their efforts were in vain. The Third and Fifteenth Army suffered extreme losses and the Fourth Army could not be salvaged. It was pushed back to the frontier of East Prussia and finally forced to save itself by passing the German frontier. "Thus our magnificent operation which made the capitals of almost every European country tremble came to an end," wrote Tuchatchevsky.

Nevertheless, the Battle of Warsaw did not become a Cannae, for the simple reason that the forces of Marshal Pilsudski were too weak. Moreover there were no speedy units on the right Polish flank to overtake the Russians and to cut off their retreat. The entire Russian western army group could have been encircled or pushed against the German frontier if the Polish right wing had possessed greater mobility and speed than it actually had. But even so, the Polish victory was decisive. The Russian troops which escaped the Polish pursuit according to Tuchatchevsky himself, reached the line Grodno-Volkovysk "in a lamentable state." The Russo-Polish War was decided on the Vistula. The Battle of the Niemen which took place at a later date was nothing but an aftermath of the victorious Polish counter-offensive.

BASIC PRINCIPLE INAPPLICABLE

Our survey of recent wars revealed the singular fact that, in the period of mass-armies, it was rarely possible to apply the basic principle of warfare and to concentrate superior masses at the decisive point. That the concentration of vast numbers in one sector should be particularly difficult, in spite of our modern transport facilities, is certainly a paradox. There is hardly any doubt that World War I could have been decided on several occasions if the principle of concentration had been applied. The failure to exploit strategic opportunities by quick concentrations must be attributed to many and different causes.

Many promising opportunities were lost as a consequence of errors of judgment, such as those on the German side in the Battle of Mons and Namur. Sometimes the surprise could not be accomplished because the attacked party prematurely detected the intentions of its opponent and was able to take timely precautions, as did the Russians late in 1914 when they frustrated the Austro-German advance to the middle Vistula. It is true that errors of judgment and unsuccessful surprise moves happen in any war and are by no means typical only of World War I. It is, however, characteristic of that war that decisive results were not even accomplished in those instances where the opponent was surprised and had himself contributed to the surpriser's victory. In such cases, full success was not achieved because the surprise was not utilised for developing numerical superiority at the decisive point, as happened in the Battle of the Marne in September, 1914, and during the offensive of Lodz in the autumn of the same year.

What is the reason for these repeated failures to utilize successful surprise for strategic concentration? The military leaders of World War I realised of course, the necessity of forming a centre of gravity at the point of attack. Most of their actions certainly served the idea of strategic concentration. Yet in practice, they were unable to concentrate sufficient masses at the decisive point. It appears thus that under modern conditions concentration of large forces is much more difficult than in previous wars. Before

World War I, doubts had been expressed whether operations with an army of millions would be as easy as with the typical nineteenth century army of one hundred thousand men.

To many soldiers, the conduct of an army of several millions appeared as an insoluble problem. This view was strongly opposed by Count von Schlieffen. "It is true," he wrote, "that the command of an army was always an extremely difficult enterprise, whether the army was small or big. But it will be hard to prove that the difficulties of military leadership increase in the same proportion as the numbers of armies.

Schlieffen repeatedly discussed the question of how the enemy's flank should be attacked. His answer was: "Not with one or two corps, *but with one or several armies.* The attack of these armies should not be directed against the enemy's wing, but against his line of retreat." He admitted, however, that only a military genius would dare take the risk of moving all, or the largest part, of his forces against the enemy's flank, let alone operate in the enemy's rear. His own war plan against France is an example for such a risk.

DEFENCE ACQUIRES STRENGTH

The principle of concentration is more important in our time than it ever was before, for the simple reason that defence has acquired a technical strength unknown in previous periods and that, moreover, defence quickly increases its power during battle, while the power of attack diminishes. Consequently, only the commander has a chance of winning a decisive victory who, *by surprise,* is able to concentrate an almost *incredible* numerical superiority at the centre of the battle. This superiority must be so overwhelming that the organisation of the enemy army is immediately crushed.

Moreover, the numerical superiority must be maintained throughout the entire operation without ever giving the opponent a chance to re-establish quantitative equilibrium. Schlieffen proposed to carry out attacks on the enemy flanks with some twenty corps. This figure is certainly not a fantastic exaggeration. A striking force of that size is an absolute necessity if a victory of annihilation shall be won against a modern mass-army.[7]

Such thoughts clearly oppose many uses of modern linear strategy which, on the whole, is the result rather of technical progress than of the numerical increase of armies. The armies of the Russo-Polish War in 1920 were not larger than those of the last century, yet linear strategy was applied in this war still more than in World War I.

The importance of terrain is being rated more highly since 1914 than by the classical writers of the last century. The maxim "hold whatever you have and never abandon a foot of ground which you won," was regarded by General von Falkenhayn as a new truth "beyond any doubt." Certainly, this doctrine would not have found the approval of Napoleon, Lee, Moltke, nor of Schlieffen who had taught the exact opposite: "It is better to abandon a whole province than to divide an army."

Schlieffen clearly recognised that especially in the period of mass-armies, *strategy of annihilation is only possible by continuous movement.* Only by movement can rigid fronts be avoided. It is possible that Falkenhayn spoke more as a politician than as a soldier and a strategist. He who does not abandon terrain, usually obeys political pressure, but rarely follows strategic consideration.[8]

The tendency to fill large spaces with a limited number of troops in linear deployment, a tendency which made its appearance in World War I, Certainly does not correspond to the opinions of the military classics.

Modern equipment makes it possible to protect vast expanses by weak forces. This fact may be used as a favourable argument for the division and dispersion of force which in former times would have invited disaster. Unfortunately, technical progress strengthened the old inclination to divide military forces according to unconscious sentiments and "traditional manners without knowing why." (Clausewitz). Such habits are dangerous because they may prevent the concentration of sufficient numbers.

Since it is impossible to attack everywhere on a broad front, the forms of fighting must differ on various sectors. Attack requires incomparably more force than defence. Therefore strictest economy of force must prevail on all sectors where no attacks take place. Schlieffen propounded the rule of diverting to all secondary fronts "as much French forces as possible by as few German forces as possible."

SACRIFICES MUST BE MADE

This rule still holds good today; the unimportant fronts, or at least those fronts where the decisive battle is not being fought, must make sacrifices for the sake of the decisive front. Consequently, the maxim "never abandon any ground" is not valid with respect to secondary fronts. If one wishes to win a conclusive victory, one should not scatter one's forces in order to hold unimportant terrain, nor protect areas of lesser importance.

The annihilation of the enemy army is the only objective, not the defence of localities or regions. Also today, in the period of mass-armies, there is "no higher and, simpler strategic law than: Hold together all your forces." (Clausewitz). This sounds easy, indeed. Yet the history of war proves that only a Titan is able to apply this seemingly simple principle. He who will win everything, must dare staking everything on one single card. By doing so, a military genius does not act like a gambler. He acts rather as a serenely self-confident and bold personality who is inspired by the "sacred fire" of the will to win and who aspires to the highest success.

To concentrate overwhelmingly superior numbers at the decisive points is impossible without strategic surprise. The assembly of the shock-group must therefore be done as quickly as possible in such a way that all units can attack at one and the same time. "The more the concentration can be compressed into one act and one moment, the more perfect are its results." (Clausewitz). To use one's forces "in driblets," as for instance, during the *course à la mer* or during the offensive of Lodz, must be avoided by all means. Only a complete ad quick concentration makes possible an attack which, like a mighty avalanche, overwhelms the surprised opponent and everything that is put in its path.

There is little reason to doubt the possibility of a modern battle of annihilation according to the model of Cannae, provided all necessary conditions are fulfilled. This opinion cannot be invalidated by the fact that in recent wars only one perfect Cannae, the Battle of Tannenberg and only one near-Cannae, the Battle of Warsaw, were won. For also in former times an entirely successful battle of annihilation was extremely rare. Two thousand years passed after the Battle of Cannae until at Sedan in 1940 a new Cannae was won.

In the lengthy period between these two battles numerous incomplete battles of annihilation were fought and they usually occurred at historic turning points. If in a future war, a commander will appear with all the qualities of Hannibal, then a perfect masterpiece in the art of war, that is to say a battle of Cannae, may again succeed. It would be preposterous and dangerous to deny such a possibility. The essence and nature of war arc best understood if one supposes that war always tends to reach its extreme. This happens when "the idea of war is realised, by an efficient army and an independent will." (Clausewitz).

NOTES

1. Difficulties of pursuit: During the Battle of France pursuit was most effectively undertaken by the German army. The reason was that the German army had overwhelming lire power and that, due to mechanisation and motorisation, its average speed was superior to the speed of the French army. This superiority was however exceptional. General Erfurth's arguments are still valid in the case of more or less equal armament and motorisation on both sides. The war in Russia and North Africa has shown that effective pursuit soon comes on a standstill and that it is extremely difficult to overtake a beaten enemy.
2. Indecisive orders: In war one should never wait to get the best possible plan. On account of the scarcity of reliable information, the best plan is unobtainable. The most important thing is to have one plan and to adhere strictly to it, so far as possible. The function of the commander-in-chief is perhaps less to be a genius than to force his subordinates to obey the one plan which he has adopted. There is some truth in the old rule that, in war, the

simplest plan is the best. "In war so much is always unknown that it frequently happens that even the simplest actions rapidly become exceedingly complex. As from the simple to the complex is the rule in war, therefore the simpler, more direct and clearer the beginning the less likely is action to get out of hand". (Major General Fuller.)

3. Schlieffen's Idea: It must again be pointed out that such an operation with "everything one has," or with more than 20 corps as Schlieffen textually said, is not a practical, but a fantastic idea. There will be rarely enough space, or sufficient transportation for moving such a force. Nor will it be possible to move more than 20 corps around the enemy's flank secretly and speedily. Consequently no surprise will be possible if a flanking effort with such a force is attempted. The German General, Wetzell, Ludendorff's chief-of-operations, asserts that such a strategy would not have been possible during World War I, even against the Russians, let alone against the western powers.

4. French position: This statement must be taken with several grains of salt. It is undoubtedly true that the French could have attacked with stronger forces and therefore won the Battle of the Manse much more conclusively. Yet they would have been unable to use a force two or three times stronger, as Erfurth suggests. To begin with, they did not have the means of transporting such a force to the battlefield. Galliéni's army may have been small, but it appeared suddenly on the battlefield and, for this very reason, achieved a surprise which perhaps was more important for the outcome of the battle than anything else. With greater forces, Galliéni would have attacked later and in all likelihood would have been unable to surprise the Germans.

   On the other hand, the concentration of 30 to 45 divisions in the region of Paris would have dangerously weakened the French between Verdun and Belfort. The French might have won an important battle north of Paris, but they would have lost an equally important battle east of their capital. Nevertheless, the Allies on the Marne did lose an opportunity for shortening the war. In addition to stronger French forces which could have been used, there was also the theoretical possibility of having on the battlefield those English troops which still remained in Great Britain, not to mention the possibility that the British might have entered the war with a few divisions more.

5. Possibilities of Deciding World War I Earlier: The attack on the Dardanelles was one of the best chances of the Allies to win the war at an early date because, if successful, it would have made possible the supplying of Russia and moreover strong Allied operations in the Balkans against Austria. As it is well known, the attack against the Dardanelles failed because: (a) no surprise was achieved and (b) no strong forces were used. This example is therefore one of the best arguments for General Erfurth's doctrine of surprise. Incidentally, is must be noted that the Dardanelles enterprise was opposed by the British General Staff as a violation of the principle of concentration. The Allied victory in the war was certainly delayed by the refusal of orthodox soldiers to use available military strength against secondary enemies so long as the Allied

armies were not strong enough to tackle Germany herself.

6. Leadership Complex: This opinion is, however, questionable. It may be difficult to decide whether military leadership has become more "difficult", yet there is no doubt at all that it has become more complex. A modern commander has to concern himself with numerous complicated problems of which his forerunners had no idea, and there is not a single instance to show that his, task has become easier. A modern general must have an encyclopedic knowledge of modern industry, transportation, economics, sociology, etc. which in former times was certainly not required. To the end of the 18th century, a military commander did not even need a general staff and could issue orders "on sight". At present, he relies on a whole academy of scientifically trained officers and the general staff has still a tendency to grow. The complexity of modern warfare has given rise to a strong military bureaucracy which, though indispensable, in turn increases the difficulties of command. The "decline" of generalship must partly be attributed to the complexity of modern war.
7. Fantastic Figures: It must again be pointed out that this figure is fantastic. There will be available rarely enough means of transport for the concentration of such a force. Neither can such a force be moved secretly, nor with appropriate speed, so that "concentration of 20 corps" and "surprise" are incompatible notions. For all practical purposes, the rule should read as follows: Attack with the maximum of force which you can quickly and secretly transport. There is an optimum size for an attacking force which is a product of, or a compromise between, transport capacity, maneuvering space, fire power, mobility and secrecy. Fire superiority is a relative term and dependent upon the enemy's lire power at the point of attack.
8. Value of Terrain: This statement certainly requires qualification. The value of terrain is not equal everywhere; on the contrary, there is terrain, the conquest of which has decisive importance. Erfurth's opinion is entirely justified in the case of, comparatively speaking, useless terrain. Falkenhayn could indeed have abandoned parts of conquered Belgium terrain and thereby have improved his position. The Russians, repeatedly in their history, relinquished vast territory without impairing their situation, while retreats in the desert usually even improve the situation of the retreating army (shortening of supply lines).

   Yet it is entirely different with other kinds of terrain. The French in 1914, abandoned the iron ore mines of Briey and Longwy and this turned out to be one of the major causes why Germany could maintain her military strength for four years, while France had difficulties in equipping her army. It is also obvious that the loss of Paris, of the use of the Suez Canal and the Caucaus was of a decisive nature for France, Great Britain and Russia respectively, but not the loss of Arras, of El Alamein or of Odessa. To be sure, the main goal in war is the destruction of the enemy army and not the conquest of territory. Yet the strength of the enemy army is dependent upon some parts of territory, the loss of which may have the same effect as the defeat of the enemy in open battle.

VII

Surprise, War of Position; Attack

During World War I, both sides tried to overcome the war of position and to restore the war of movement. In the first years of this struggle, the importance of terrain was overstressed. Consequently, it was never attempted to regain liberty of movement by voluntary retreats. The resumption of the war of movement was chiefly attempted by a break-through of enemy fronts. The break-through, in turn, required tactical victory. In the course of this war tactical victories were often won and appropriate methods had been developed to master the intricate tactical problems of modern war. Yet this was only the first step. The second step, by far the more important, was to find a method of developing tactical into strategic success. This proved to be an extremely difficult task which was accomplished only under exceptionally favourable conditions.

Imposed by particular conditions of the war of position, preparations for attack were frequently prematurely discovered by the opponent; attacks seldom came unexpectedly. The selection of the point of attack was usually conditioned by the situation in general and by the shape of the front in particular. This is especially true of the offensive projects of the Entente which usually could be deduced beforehand. The Central Powers had the advantage of inner lines and were therefore in a better position to surprise their opponents since they had a certain liberty of choke where to strike. A central position may be an advantage at the beginning of a war because it facilitates the formation of a centre of gravity; in a war of position, it also facilitates strategic surprise.

In the first years of World War I, the Central Powers took full advantage of inner lines and attacked on various fronts. They lost the advantage of the central position during the last year of that conflict. After fighting had ceased on the eastern front, Germany and Austria were left only with the alternate choice of attacking either in France or in Italy. The conditions of the Italian front were not altogether favourable for large scale operations. Consequently, the big German offensive during the first part of 1918 was not unexpected by the French and British. The Germans could therefore accomplish only tactical surprise, and tried to keep secret the strength of their offensive, the exact point of attack and the time of its start.

To screen the preparations for a big offensive is much more difficult in a war of position than in a war of movement. The front lines are very close together and the intelligence service finds many indications which reveal any kind of unusual activity, however well hidden. Since the secrecy of offensive preparations is a dubious affair, surprise should have been attempted by speeding up the execution of the offensive plan. But speed was made very difficult by the fact that frontal attacks against a modern defensive system which is equipped with most powerful and numerous defensive weapons, requires an immense amount of military strength. Numerous units and immense quantities of weapons must be brought to the point of attack and be deployed before the operation. This preparation lasts, of course, for a considerable period. Thorough preparation and speed exclude each other.

SURPRISE IMPORTANT IN BREAK-THROUGH

We shall discuss a few examples from World War I and examine the importance of surprise for break-through operations in a war of position. We shall also examine whether Clausewitz's principle to utilize surprise for gaining relative superiority at the decisive point was followed as it should have been.

The offensive methods employed by the French during the winter battle in the Champagne (February to March, 1915) show many deficiencies which are characteristic of World War I methods. The greatest deficiency was the complete lack of any kind of surprise. Already at the end of December, 1914, the German Third Army reported that a French offensive in the Champagne was imminent. These reports were confirmed by secret agents. The French were as yet unexperienced in the subtle art of camouflaging military preparations. They were extremely active in the sectors where they intended to attack and openly built up their assault positions. Their intentions were betrayed to the Germans by visible lively activity in the French trenches. Moreover, the French General Staff hoped by several partial attacks to exhaust the Germans before the beginning of the main operation. This tactic, of course, only warned the Germans who finally knew everything about the French plan, including the date of attack. The result of the offensive was necessarily disappointing for the military leaders of the Entente. After the failure of the first onslaught, the battle degenerated into protracted and inconclusive lighting. The French maintained a heavy artillery fire against the German positions and launched many smaller attacks by day as well as by night in the vain hope of achieving a break-through.

The course of this offensive suggested that any offensive should be concentrated into one main effort and that the success of an offensive operation is dependent upon speed and the power of the first blow. Frontal attacks require a very substantial superiority on the part of the attacker. If numerical superiority cannot be established, the offensive peters Out into successive blows which become increasingly weaker without yielding any appreciable result. Victory at the decisive point alone is important and compensates for any losses which may occur on secondary fronts. Consequently, the fronts where no decisions are being sought, should be manned with a minimum of force.[1] Everything has to be subordinated to the intention of bringing "the maximum of force into battle" at the decisive point. It is a law that heavy blows must be concentrated in space and time. All the advantages of surprise are sacrificed if one attempts to reach victory not by one big blow, but by several simultaneous and successive actions. An insufficient effort not only leads to failure, but usually to damage (Clausewitz). An offensive which has been stopped can rarely be started again.

ATTACK! ATTACK! ATTACK!

The French generalissimo took these lessons into account, when he launched his next offensive (spring battle in Artois, 1915). He prescribed that the attack should be continued without respite until the objective was reached. Reinforcements were to be continuously brought up to the first lines. In the battle of Artois, the Entente used superior forces at the decisive point at the same time and for one single operation. But the question must be asked whether they also brought the maximum of numerical force into battle. The answer is a clear negative. Clausewitz's "first principle of strategy" was not adhered to by the High Command of the Allies.

Between May 9 and June 18, 33 infantry divisions of the British First Army and the French Tenth Army tried in vain to drive 20 German infantry divisions from their positions. Looking at the relation of total infantry strength on the entire western theatre of war, it appears that the Allies in June 1915; had altogether a superiority of around 600 battalions. They were therefore much stronger than the German army. If they had complied with the doctrine of Clausewitz, they would have concentrated far greater forces for their offensive in Artois. In this case, the Germans probably would have been unable to prevent a break-through of their lines because even with, comparatively speaking, the small forces which the Allies actually led into combat, the Allies succeeded in opening a gap of four miles in the German front. They also took a large part of the Loretto Hill. The Germans were thus confronted by a serious crisis.

These initial successes of the Entente were largely due to the surprise which this time the French had been able to accomplish. Their troops had been drawn up so skillfully that the Germans did not realize the impending danger. Fire-preparation had been compressed into a few hours. Repeated intervals in the heavy artillery fire deceived the Germans about the time of the assault. When the operation finally started, the German command and troops were caught by surprise.

On the contrary, the preparations of the British did not remain hidden from the Germans. They deployed so openly that the "German flyers had almost an exact blue-print of the offensive the British were preparing" (Krafft von Dellmensingen.) No wonder that the British attack failed on the entire line.

ENVELOPMENT SHOULD HAVE BEEN EASY

On the whole, the Allied offensive was a failure, although the Allies had many advantages on their side and the shape of the German line would have made an envelopment comparatively easy. Surprise and superiority made initial successes possible. But the battle did not develop into a decisive victory, chiefly because coordination and cooperation between the separate units of the Allied forces were deficient. To overcome the tenacious defence of the German troops, who continued to resist even in the most desperate situations, a greater numerical superiority than the Allies actually mustered at the beginning of the battle would have been necessary.

But the military leaders of the Entente still were far from grasping the essential problem. In their next big offensive (autumn battle in Artois and in the Champagne) they attempted to break the German lines by an artillery preparation of unprecedented intensity. The French High Command hoped to break German resistance by a mass-fire of many days for which immense quantities of ammunition had been made ready. They did not bother about surprise. In the offensive sector, the French had brought up their first trenches as near to the German lines as possible. The assault trenches were considerably lengthened and increased. Precautions were taken for the assembly of large forces. All these preparations were, of course, easily discovered by German flyers. Their reports enabled the German Command to forecast correctly the details of the French offensive.

The British, on the other hand, had in the meantime learned the rudiments of the art of camouflage. Though their preparations in Artois were similar to those of the French in the Champagne, it was much more difficult to deduce their true intentions.

The double offensive of the Entente aimed at a strategic break-through. It was undertaken on a sufficiently broad front and with strong force In addition, the conditions on the side of the defender favoured the plans of the Allies, for the German High Command was not prepared for the Franco-British offensive. Up to the last moment, General von Falkenhayn refused to believe in a serious attempt at a break-through, although the Allies had not at all concealed their intentions and While the commanders of the threatened German armies had repeatedly asked for reinforcements in order to forestall the imminent danger. Falkenhayn was convinced that the enemy was merely feinting. Even the intense Allied artillery preparation and the increase of air activity could not shake his belief. Falkenhayn rated the moral power of the Allies, and particularly of the French, as poor and did not consider them capable of a strong military effort. His attitude is an impressive example of the frequent incredulity of senior commanders with respect to justified warnings of subordinate officers.

RISK IN DENYING THE OBVIOUS

As a result, the enemy achieved a surprise which he had taken no trouble to prepare. The preparatory artillery fire started on September 22. But only on September 25, when the German Third and Sixth Army had reported the launching of an enemy offensive, did General von Falkenhayn cease to deny the obvious. The seriousness of the situation was no longer doubtful. Few reserves were available and they were far from the menaced fronts. It was therefore highly questionable whether the enemy offensive could be stopped. Falkenhayn, however, was lucky because some German forces returning from the eastern front arrived in Belgium in time to bolster the weak German defences. But even with these reinforcements, there was a considerable danger not only that the German defenders would be pushed back for some miles, but that their lines would be completely crushed. The numerical superiority of the attacker should have sufficed for an important victory.

Although the importance of the surprise factor was considerable in all Allied offensives in 1915, the Allies, astonishingly enough, neglected it in their operations during 1916 and 1917. The French generalissimo thought that the maximum of material force, in particular that of artillery fire, applied on a front as broad as possible was the surest way to victory. In addition, the importance of neutralizing or destroying the enemy's reserves was recognised. The Allies no longer believed in the possibility of achieving a break-through by one single operation, but thought that it required several successive offensives. With painful efforts and an immense amount of work and material, the western powers through, many months systematically prepared the Battle of the Somme. They staked everything on an overwhelming artillery assault and entirely disregarded the element of surprise. Consequently, the Germans had sufficient advance knowledge of the coming Franco-British attack.

By May 26, 1916, the commander of the German Second Army had gained the impression that the British were preparing an offensive north of the Somme. On June 2 the same Army reported the aggravation of the situation on its right flank. A big British offensive seemed to be impending. During the course of June it became apparent that the French were preparing to participate with considerable force in the British offensive, despite the still raging Battle of Verdun which tied up strong French forces. By the middle of June it was definitely established that the French had taken over a part of the British front north of the Somme.

It is hard to explain why General von Falkenhayn did not sufficiently reinforce the threatened front, especially since enough reserves were available for strengthening the Second Army. General van Falkenhayn made a very economical use of the German reserves before and during the Battle of the Somme, possibly because lie planned to decide the war in the west by a German counter-offensive after the British had exhausted themselves by the Somme offensive. He was also thrifty, because the German reserves had been reduced by the Battle of Verdun and by General Brussilov's offensive on the Russian front. This scarcity of reserves may be the main reason why the German High Command did not take appropriate measures to transform the Battle of the Somme into a German victory.

BETTER FIGHTING THAN LEADERSHIP

The Allies began their offensive with a preparatory artillery assault of seven days. This effort dispelled any doubts about the violence of the impending storm, but it did not change Falkenhayn's dispositions. When on July 1 the Franco-British attack broke only seven German divisions, already reduced by the Allied artillery assault, faced fourteen British and five French divisions. The Allied offensive was thus undertaken under particularly favourable circumstances, chiefly because the

German defenders had failed to take the necessary precautionary measures and to reinforce the menaced sector of their front in time. Nevertheless, the western powers did not achieve the coveted break-through. But this result must be ascribed less to the skill of the German leadership than to the fighting qualities of the German troops.

Every subsequent Allied offensive in 1917 was planned according to the pattern of the Battle of the Somme which was the first battle of materiel in history. Summarizing the lessons of the Battle of the Somme, the French *Grand Quartier General* acknowledged the importance of surprising the enemy by the first blows of an offensive. This sound principle was, however, not utilised when the offensives of 1917 were being planned. Perhaps, the French did not properly understand the conditions necessary for strategic surprise. They did not believe in the chances of an offensive without an artillery preparation of several days, though obviously the artillery assault served as a warning signal for the opponent and precluded any real surprise.

Shortly before the start of the French offensive in the spring of 1917, General Nivelle became French generalissimo. He was little favoured by luck. First of all, the weather upset his calculations. His artillery preparations of seven days had to be prolonged, because storm, rain and snow made exact fire impossible. The French infantry attack did not begin on April 12, as originally intended, but on April 14.

The Germans had known of the impending French offensive since the middle of February. In the course of March, photographic reconnaissance showed many changes in the French positions in front of the German Third and Seventh Army which indicated offensive intentions on the part of the French. Prisoners confirmed these suspicions. On April 4, during an attack northwest of Heims, important documents were captured which contained exact information of the preparations for an offensive on the Aisne. Some months previous, on December 16, 1916, a new French regulation on offensive tactics had also been captured by the Germans who therefore knew everything about the French methods. Thus, the Germans had enough time and opportunity to make thorough defensive preparations.

Nivelles offensive ended in a serious French defeat. Many reasons have been advanced for Nivelle's failure. But all critics are agreed that its essential cause was the complete lack of surprise.

The British offensive around Arras which took place almost at the same time was not more successful. Also in this case, the

Germans had advance knowledge of the British intentions. They rightly deduced the exact location of the British attack and could consequently take all necessary precautions.

MATERIEL AS A FACTOR

The concept of the battle of materiel is to defeat the opponent by crushing material superiority without relying on generalship. It found its extreme expression in the British offensive in Flanders in the summer and fall of 1917. The war industries of the western powers and the United States had mobilised to their full capacity to crush German resistance. In the second half of June, 1917, the German command expected a big British offensive in Flanders. The Germans also knew against which sector of their positions the onslaught would be directed. They lacked only knowledge of the date of the British attack, but the British artillery preparations did not fail to provide them with this bit of important information. The British bombardment lasted from July 22 to 31. The subsequent British attack yielded only moderate results which, despite continuous and repeated efforts and attacks of the majority of the engaged British formations, could not be improved. By August 25 the first round of the gigantic struggle came to a standstill.

Altogether the great Battle of Flanders raged more than one hundred days. It only confirmed the former experience that a break-through either succeeds quickly or never.

After the failure of these offensives, the Allies adopted a new theory, according to which a gigantic single blow was to be replaced by continuous partial attacks with limited objectives. It should have been dear, however, that such technique could not yield important results. The new doctrine was in flagrant contradiction of Clausewtz's principle that all forces which are earmarked and available for one strategic purpose, should be used simultaneously. The idea of a continuous battle of attrition in Flanders and on the Somme did not provide a solution for the tactical difficulties of the break-through.

The numerous Allied offensives until the Battle of Flanders conclusively proved the indispensability of surprise. Surprise and concentration are, and remain, the main conditions for any tactical and strategical success. The break-through in the war of position is undoubtedly the most difficult form of attack. It cannot be accomplished without surprise, the purpose of which is to prevent the defender from organizing his defences and bringing up his reserves. If the offensive fails in its initial phases, its continuation against an alert and warned enemy has not the slightest chance. Up to the Battle of Flanders in 1917 the western powers had found no solution for the difficult task of breaking through a front defended with modern weapons.

The German military leaders merit the credit of having developed an efficient method of attack in the war of position. For them, surprise was the starting point of all their planning.

SURPRISE IN OFFENSIVE TECHNIQUE

In a small engagement near Vailly on October 31, 1914, and on November 2 near Soupir, both of which had only local importance, the Germans made their first experiments for developing appropriate offensive methods. The same technique was later employed in the Battle of Soissons during January, 1915. The methods of Vailly, Soupir and Soissons were improved by the Germans and became the basis of all their later break-through operations. The essential idea was to surprise the enemy. The German technique was always effective, provided the enemy had been surprised. On the contrary, it always failed when surprise could not be accomplished and when the enemy had been able to take timely precautions. Surprise, it cannot longer be doubted, is the condition *sine qua non* of any offensive technique.

The Russians by April 12, 1915, had already rather accurate information about the Austro-German preparations for an attack in the area of Gorlice. They believed the Germans would bring up strong reinforcements to counter the Russian offensive in the Carpathians. They had also gathered indications of a coming

German attack against the centre of the Russian Third Army which, if successful, would hit the right flank of those Russian units which had advanced beyond the ridge of the Carpathians. The attack of Gorlice-Tarnov was therefore not a complete surprise, although the Russians ignored one essential point: the participation of German units in the operation. Curiously enough, the Russians despite their knowledge and the increasing amount of incoming information, did nothing to strengthen their menaced front.

Already in 1914, the Russian secret service functioned poorly. For instance, the shifting of an entire German army from southern Poland to the vicinity of Thorn remained unnoticed. But in the spring of 1915 the performance of the Russian secret service was even worse. The Russian High Command failed to learn to which sector of the eastern front the German forces had been transported from the west. They received many contradictory reports of the location of these German units and were therefore unable to gain a reliable picture.

The Germans, of course, had spared no efforts to confuse the Russians. They circulated false information of strong German concentrations in East Prussia. In addition, they skillfully screened their railway transports from the west. The three railroads to Eastern Prussia were crowded with numerous trains. The troops which were to go to eastern Galicia were first transported or the railroads leading to East Prussia; their trains were re-directed to Galicia only from the most advanced railroad junctions. The assembly on the Galician front was made in such a way that Russian air reconnaissance did not gather any information. German officers who reconnoitered the enemy positions wore Austrian uniforms.

In contrast to the technique of the western powers, the German artillery preparation was compressed within a few hours. The leader of the Russian Third Army realised the imminence of a strong attack on his forces only a very short time before the attack actually began. (May 1, 1915). On the morning of the next day, he received some reinforcements. They were not sufficient to prevent the collapse of his front. Part of the reinforcements arrived too late.

VERDUN ATTACK BELATED

The German attack on Verdun in February, 1916, was strangely influenced by the element of surprise. For the first time during the war, multiple preparations for a difficult offensive had been concealed from the enemy; in particular the concentration of large artillery forces and of an immense quantity of ammunition. The importance of secrecy had been strongly emphasised by the German High Command and every detail was carried out as secretly as possible. In order to deceive the enemy, the Germans prepared sham attacks on several other sectors of the western front.

These precautions were effective. If the Germans had really attacked on February 12, as it was originally intended, they would have encountered an incompletely prepared opponent. The French on the afternoon of February 10 received a report from a "very reliable source" announcing the German offensive. Within two days the menaced front of Verdun could not be reinforced. On February 12, the positions around Verdun were held only by five French divisions. One of the most important sectors of this front was defended by a wholly insufficient force; one division approached the front, but was still lagging far behind. Against this weakly defended sector alone, the Germans had concentrated seven and one-half infantry divisions, six of which had just arrived at the front.

All conditions seemed to be favourable for the German offensive against Verdun. Yet the weather came to the assistance of the French. Visibility was impaired by torrential rains and thick fog. The offensive, at first planned as a lightning attack, was postponed for one day. The weather did not improve and the offensive finally started on February 21. In this period, the French were able to make up for all the deficiencies of their defence organisation. Moreover, they received additional information of the German plan and could therefore take all necessary measures. The defenders of Verdun on February 21 were ready for the German attack.

The postponement of the German offensive against Verdun proved to be fatal. The question has often been discussed whether this postponement was really unavoidable. Opinions are divided. But even assuming that as a consequence of bad weather effective artillery preparation was out of question, it is certainly hard to approve the decision to wait passively for ten long days and then to launch the offensive in rigorously the same disposition, with the same strength and according to the same plan as that upon which it was to be started ten days before.

Surprise cannot be accomplished after so long a delay. Yet the success of the Verdun offensive was dependent upon initial surprise and extreme speed. The German High Command could not expect that the French would remain inactive during ten long days and do nothing to strengthen their defence.[2] Consequently, the attacker had to do everything possible to increase, the power of his own attack. If this was not practical, there remained no other alternative but to renounce the whole enterprise. To be sure, this would have been an extremely difficult decision, but it was preferable to the useless expenditure of valuable strength upon an impossible task. The long battle of Verdun only confirmed the old experience that a break-through operation which fails at the start, might better be discontinued.

From their own and from the experience of the Allies the German leaders had concluded that the time of artillery preparation of an offensive should be still further shortened, if surprise was to be accomplished. The preparation for the Battle of Verdun began only a few hours before the attack was launched. The Central Powers steadily improved their artillery technique. Their later offensives were characterised by artillery preparation in minimum time which was supplemented by many tricks to deceive the enemy. This improved technique led to the victories in the fall of 1917 in Italy and in the first half of 1918 in France.

CADORNA'S THEORY OF CAPORETTO

The question whether the Italian defeat at Karfeit (Caporetto) was the result of successful surprise has been widely discussed. It is controversial whether the Austro-German offensive on the Isonzo in 1917 began with strategic or only a tactical surprise. General Cadorna, then Italian generalissimo, ascribes the collapse of his army less to the efficiency of the attacker than to the poor morale of the Italians. There is little doubt that the Italians themselves contributed to their defeat, quite in accordance with Schlieffen's doctrine relating to the necessary conditions for a battle of annihilation. It is also true that many special circumstances favoured the success on the Isonzo. The German attack began at the worst possible moment for the Italians. Besides, the Germans counted upon the fact that the fog which at that season prevails in the higher altitudes would prevent the Italian from observing the activity in the valleys. This assumption proved to be correct. Merit and luck on the part of the attacker paralleled weakness on the part of the defender.

The Battle of Karfreit is a classical example of Clausewita's assertion that surprise may have independent intellectual effects beyond its purely military consequences. Many Italian units fought with great bravery. Nevertheless, confusion and lack of courage quickly infected the bulk of the Italian army and caused its virtual disintegration.[3] This twelfth battle of the Isoozo also proved Clausewitz's tenet: "Only he can surprise who imposes his law on the enemy." The Austro-German armies possessed the initiative throughout the entire battle. The Italians were unable to liberate themselves from their intellectual subjection to the enemy's measures and to regain their physical liberty of movement and decision.

In the preparation of the German offensive in March, 1918, the experiences of the Battle of Karfreit and of the tank battle of Cambrai in November and December, 1917, were taken into account. The German counter-attack of November 30, 1917, near Cambrai had been successful chiefly because the Germans were forced to compress their preparations within live to six days. Hence the preparations for the great offensive in March, 1918, were reduced to the extreme minimum. In the meantime the German Captain, Pulkowski, had invented an artillery technique which made it possible to begin directly with destruction-fire without previous range testing. This invention seemed to be the "lacking keystone for an effective system of surprise" (General von Kuhl). In addition, every precaution was taken to conceal from the enemy preparations for the offensive. Confusion and deception were systematically applied in most minute detail. Still the enemy was not entirely fooled. After the Russian collapse, the military and political leaders of the Entente counted firmly upon an energetic German attempt to win the war before the American army could intervene on the European battlefields. During the winter months, the tension in Paris grew constantly. The French press conjectured upon the direction and strength of the expected German attack.

HAIG EXPECTED ATTACK

The German High Command did everything possible to screen its projects. A plan of deception was drawn up for the entire western front in order to make the Allies believe in a German offensive between Rheims and the Argonne, or in the vicinity of Verdun, and to reassure them of the safety of the British sector.[4] Nevertheless, Field Marshal Haig realised soon enough that the main German effort would be directed against his own front. As early as March 2, he expressed this opinion to the commanders of the different British armies. The presence in front of the British lines of the German Generals von Hutier and von Bulow, both reputed to be offensive specialists, confirmed Haig. On the other hand, extensive preparation behind the German lines in the Champagne suggested an offensive in that area. General Pétain steadfastedly believed that the Germans would concentrate their main blow against the French lines. However, shortly before the German offensive, the British came into possession of reliable information. Their secret service and their air reconnaissance did good work. The depositions of prisoners, and deserters of Alastian and Polish origin, removed the last doubts. It only remained dubious whether the German attack on the British lines would not be supplemented by another operation, possibly in the Champagne.

British military historians bared many different reasons for the severe British defeat in March, 1918, such as insufficient numerical strength of the British positions. The commander of the British Fifth Army also lacked reserves. One British corps had retreated without any apparent reason because its commander had interpreted his orders erroneously. Indeed, there is little doubt that British generalship assisted the German army and made many precious contributions to the German victory.[5] Yet the surprise which was successfully effected by the Germans must be considered as the essential factor of that victory. Since October-November, 1914, that is to say, after the first Battle of Ypres, the British had fought no defensive battle. They still clung to their outmoded rigid linear-defence system and were being thoroughly taken aback by the newly developed efficient German offensive technique. Churchill was entirely right when he pointed out that the British were being surprised by the violence, the extent and the strength of the German attack. This explains the enormous intellectual consequences which followed the German blow and which almost paralysed the resistance of the British Fifth Army. But chance also Intervened to the disadvantage of the British. The morning of March 21, 1918, was particularly foggy. The British troops were practically blindfolded for a long time and were unable to use the most important defensive weapon in their possession, the machine gun. Chance thus made the German assault technique much more effective than could ever have been foreseen.

The German March offensive had, however, one particular weakness: the Germans attacked at only one sector. Deceptive information, sham movements and other ruses could not divert the Allied reserves, let alone neutralize them. In order to prevent the enemy reserves from intervening in the battle, they had to be pinned down by strong secondary attacks on distant fronts. Whether forces could have been, made available for such a purpose, is another question. Yet the previous offensives of the Entente showed that even a successful break-through cannot strategically be exploited unless the enemy-reserves are neutralised. A break-through attempt against the centre of a broad front is the most difficult of all attacks, since the defender can bring up his reserves from both sides and thus compensate for the numerical superiority of the attacker before the decision has fallen. Only a very heavy numerical superiority can counterbalance this advantage for the defender. The German offensive gained considerable initial successes, but its strong power was prematurely exhausted.

ALLIES' INITIAL SURPRISE

The Allies accomplished their first surprise in November 1917, when the British unexpectedly attacked on a quiet front. A new technique of attack was the main feature of the British success near Cambrai. For the first time, the infantry assault was not prepared by artillery, but by tanks, which also for the first time were used in considerable quantity. The attack broke with a suddenness hitherto unknown. The technique of Cambrai was refined and used in all later offensive and counter-offensive operations of the Entente. The tank provided the western powers with an offensive weapon superior to anything the Germans had developed up to the end of the war.

The Franco-American counter-offensive of July 18, 1918, and the Franco-British attack of August 8, 1918, did not surprise the German soldiers on the battlefield, but the German High Command. This must be emphasised if the right conclusions are to be drawn from these operations. Before July 1918, the Germans already had been told by reliable agents and deserters of the presence of strong enemy concentrations in the forest of Villers-

Cotterets. They were specifically warned that an enemy-attack between the Aisne and the Marne was imminent. The German troops did everything to improve their defences. The High Command expected an Allied offensive by July 15. When this offensive failed to materialize it was assumed that, as a consequence of the then proceeding German offensive on both sides of Rheims, the Allies had no force available for this operation. This optimism was not shared by the troops of the menaced front who were ready for the enemy when he attacked on July 18; as ready as was possible in the weak German positions and with the insufficient strength of their garrisons.

Again the German troops reported about enemy offensive preparations at the beginning of August, 1918. On August 3 pronounced sound of motors in movement were noticed which disclosed the imminence of an enemy tank attack from the region of Villers-Bretonneux. These reports were laid to imagination and nerves. Nothing was done to improve the German tank defences in that sector.

A German flyer on August 6 discovered about one hundred tanks in front of the German Second Army. The commander of this army received this information from his superior authorities, although, characteristically, without comment. The German High Command, the commander of the army group and even the commander of the Second Army did not believe in the possibility of a strong enemy offensive until on August 8 a gigantic blow smashed the front of the Second Army.[6]

This strategic surprise was in part due to the enemy's mastery of the air. Nevertheless, the German High Command lacked perspicacity. They should have become suspicious after one hundred tanks had been reported near the flank of the Second Army and after two Canadian divisions had disappeared without trace from a position where they had fought for only a very short time.

The troops themselves were surprised by the Allied offensive technique. Strangely enough, the troops of the Second Army had never been informed of the experience resulting from the Battle of Cambrai and the recent battle of July 18, 1918 west of Soissons. The German High Command had not taken pains to tell the troops what to do In case the enemy attacked with tanks and without artillery preparation. It must be admitted, however, that they could not provide the troops with efficient means of counter-technique. It was impossible to furnish effective antitank weapons to the troops. And no other expedient would have been effective.

NOTES

1. Fronts and Force: This statement is correct in case there is no doubt which front is to be considered as the main front. One should not forget, however, that the earth is round and that "every road leads to Rome". It is quite possible that the enemy takes advantage of the subtle destinction between primary and secondary fronts and considers a front which we fancy to be of secondary importance as a primary front, Napoleon considered Spain as a secondary front; the collapse of Germany in 1918 began in Palestine.
   In a great war, there are many decisive points, hence many primary and only few secondary fronts. The difficulty of applying the principle of concentration is caused lust by this fact: It is almost impossible to make a neat distinction between primary and secondary fronts. One has to cover all decisive points and that may practically mean dispersion of force. It is strange that Erfurth does not realize that strategic surprise is very often the result of choosing that front which the enemy considers as secondary as one's primary front of attack. Throughout history, British strategy excelled in this kind of surprise strategy, while the continental armies usually had very rigid and narrow notions about the location of the primary front. In World War I, for instance, the Germans as well as the Entente would have had good possibilities for striking decisive blows in and through Italy. Yet neither side did, despite Caporetto which had demonstrated the strategic potentialities of the Italian front.
2. Verdun: The idea of launching a surprise attack against one of the strongest fortifications in the world sounds strange indeed. Such an attack may have been possible if the Germans, as in 1940 at Eben Emael had used new tactics and techniques. But at Verdun, the German attack, even under the most favourable circumstances, would have lasted a considerable period of time, so that the French probably would have been able to bring up their reserves at any rate. Erfurth fails to point out that the main purpose of the Verdun offensive was to bleed the French army white, and that therefore the Germans had a certain interest in prolonging the battle. This example shows that surprise should not be limited to the purely strategic field, but that in principle every strategic surprise should be combined with tactical and technical surprises. The enemy must be surprised not only by the "where?"

and "when?" but also by the "how?".

3. Surprise at Caporetto: The Battle of Caporetto is a remarkable example of surprise operations. The Italian army had suffered heavy losses in their previous offensive on the Isonzo. Therefore, their units comprised many young and unexperienced recruits. In addition, the hazard of the previous battle had left the Italians in rather unfavourable and vulnerable positions. The Austro-German armies launched their attack against the weakest parts of the Italian fort. The Italians were not prepared for an attack by the best German shock troops and had expected merely an attack from the Austrians. Moreover, the attacker employed new tactics. The main blows were delivered is the valleys, instead of across the mountains, as it was the tradition of mountain warfare. A very effective kind of artillery preparation (gas-shells) was applied, a surprise on the Italian front. Besides, the attacker was favoured by fog.

   Of course, the Italians themselves contributed to their own defeat. Once of the principal Italian commanders had been ill (or several days and was therefore unable to supervise the defence preparations. Due to a misunderstanding, the Italian artillery held back its lire until it was too late. The numerous Italian recruits became panicky when, unexpectedly, they ere attacked by gas. Had the Italians not spent a large part of their striking power in a dozen unsuccessful offensives on the Isonzo, the moral resistance of their troops would have been considerably stronger.

   Of equal importance was the panic which seized the Italian High Command when they (rained that one of the positions which they considered as vital (Monte Maggiore) had fallen. When General Cadorna received news of the fall of Monte Maggiore, he immediately ordered the retreat behind the Tagliamento and even began to make preparations for a retreat across the Piave. There is little doubt that he attached too great an importance to Monte Maggiore. The Italians could have fought on in their positions without this little fort.

   Thus the most important effect of successful surprise is the disorganisation of the enemy command. The High Command loses its control; it ignores the true situation. Orders are no longer transmitted, hence every division or even regiment makes its own decision. Besides, the general tension prevents clear and sober thinking. The degree of the defeat is overestimated and a retreat is ordered, for fear that parts of the army may be cut off and annihilated, The fall of the weak positions sweeps away the strong ones; the strong positions failed to bolster the weak.

4. Von Hutier: The British deduced the location of the German attack from an obituary in a provincial German newspaper which was signed by General von Hutier. The date-line of the obituary also indicated the place of Hutier's command. Since Hutier was the foremost German expert for offensive operations, the British had no difficulty in drawing Correct conclusions as to the sector of the German offensive.

5. Uncoordinated Command: The main reason for the German success was the

uncoordinated command of the British and French Armies. Pétain and Haig had different strategic conceptions and apprehensions, hence each placed his reserves where he thought he needed them most. The result was that the weakest spot of the entire Allied front—the joint between the French and British—remained virtually unprotected and without reserves.

6. August 8th: The surprise of August 8, 1918 was much more important and far-reaching than would appear from Erfurth's text. As a matter of fact, the German High Command believed that as a consequence of the German spring and summer offensives, the offensive power of the Allies was broken and that for a long time to come they would be unable to resume active warfare.

This dream was definitely shattered on August 8, 1918, the day which Ludendorif christened the "black day of the German Army". He realised that he himself had broken the offensive power of his own army, but not of his enemy. This intellectual surprise was at the bottom of the German capitulation. The surprised Ludendorif had lost his faculty of sober reasoning and was unable to understand how Germany could fight on the defensive. The top became panicky, and the panic spread all over the country and infected the army.

Erfurth, fur reasons of loyalty, cannot write openly and objectively on these events. Had he done so, he could have made clear that surprise has a still greater military importance than his text conveys. The successful surprise of August 8, 1918, spared the Allies at least one further year of war. Space prevents further elaboration on this point. It suffices to emphasize that time general impression, created by numerous incorrect historical accounts, according to which Germany, in November, 1918, was "finished", does not correspond to the facts. The German food supply was improving, the German submarine strength was again increasing, while the Allies were approaching a serious transport crisis. There was no *material* necessity for the Germans to capitulate. With their army and with their munition and food supply, they would have been able to continue the war, at least on the defensive. The main causes of the German collapse were of a psychological nature and the main psychological cause was the surprise bred by a realisation that the Allies were not beaten and therefore never could be beaten.

VIII

Surprise, War of Position Defence

The possibility of surprising the attacker after he has made his plan clear by his actions is one of the most important advantages of defence, according to Clausewitz. Defensive surprise requires not only a very mobile but an active defence wherever possible. After the beginning of positional warfare in the World War I, defensive battles were conducted in a different form. The defender did not fight as he should have done, for victory and for the annihilation of the opponent, but merely for his positions.

Defence was rigid and passive. By renouncing mobile and active tactics in defence one did, by the same token, renounce the advantages of surprise. For a long time the Germans clung to the peace time principle that a single line should be occupied and defended. Only gradually and slowly did they overcome this doctrine of rigid defence. After the Battle of the Somme the idea of linear defence was definitely abandoned. Hence forward defence was organised in depth and conducted in a mobile and active way. Defensive tactics again took advantage of the element of surprise.

Yet, as has been pointed out by Liddell Hart, strategic surprise in the defensive was re-discovered only at the end of the war. The main elements of classical strategy, maneuver and movement, were replaced by trench warfare. According to Marshal Pilsudski, a special "trench-psychology" had developed which exercised a strong influence on almost all military leaders in both camps. It is indeed astonishing to see how long a time it took before the strategical concepts of the World War leaders were divested of such errors arid reconciled with old and experienced truths. The strange dogma that every position, however unnecessary or unfavourable, should be defended to the very last caused many unnecessary losses and led to many belated evacuations. Heavy fighting for a locality often degenerated into a contest for mere prestige. In this case, sentiment interferes with reason and prevents arriving at appropriate decisions. World War I witnessed numerous examples of this unfortunate strategy. We may only refer to the refusal of the German High Command to evacuate the undefendable arc of Wytschaete in June, 1917. The result was a successful British surprise-attack and bloody as well as useless fighting.

Immobility of the troops and clumsiness of the leaders were the almost natural consequence of the long positional war. The easy expedient of forestalling a strong blow by a timely retreat to rear positions was rarely executed, although by such a surprise move even a thoroughly prepared offensive could have been frustrated. To evade a heavy artillery assault by with drawing the first lines to positions farther behind seems today a fairly simple device. Yet it was invented only rather recently. In March, 1917, the Germans retreated before an impending strong French offensive which, as a consequence, became a blow at a vacuum. It required a great deal of courage to break with General von Falkenhayn's principle "not to relinquish a single foot of conquered ground." Indeed, the German High Command could not carry Out this strategic retreat without encountering very serious objections of a politico-military nature.

PUBLIC OPINION FEARED

The Italian High Command Jacked the necessary boldness for a similar decision, although long before the Austro-German offensive on the Isonzo in October, 1917, in case of attack they intended to abandon their unfavourable positions and to fight the opponent from a stronger defence line. For a long time the Italians hesitated to put their plan into effect. At last it was too late to retreat successfully.

It is today hardly comprehensible why the British did not evade the extremely strong German offensive of March, 1918. When on May 26, 1918, through the deposition of two prisoners, the French were informed of the German offensive against the Chemin des Dames which was to begin two days later, they also considered a voluntary retreat because they were by no means prepared for that battle. This expedient however, was rejected tinder the pretext that it would endanger near-by positions.

In reality, the French generals were afraid of public opinion, believing that the people would not understand the abandonment without a fight of a position for which the French had made so many bloody sacrifices.[1]

The Poles, at the end of June, 1920, followed this disastrous French example. After Marshal Pilsudski had recognised that the Polish army would not be able to resist the Russian offensive, he recommended a timely and orderly retreat. General Szeptycki, one of Pilsudskis advisors, believed that a defence from prepared Polish positions would be more promising than a retreat into the open rear. Pilsudski finally agreed with him. Like the French at the Chemin des Dames, the Poles remained in their positions although they knew well what they were facing. In both cases this kind of passive defence enabled the attacker to win a considerable victory.

One of Clausewitz's main principles was never to assume a passive attitude, but to attack the front and the flank, even of an offensive enemy. According to Clausewita, the "offensive defence" should start at the very moment the enemy launches his offensive. In Clausewitz's opinion, it may sometimes be practical to retreat in order to lure the enemy into unfamiliar terrain and then to strike back from every side. Clausewita would probably have considered the German strategic retreat of March, 1917, as incomplete, since it lacked a strong surprise counterblow against the pursuing enemy.

As a matter of fact, such an operation had been discussed by the German High Command. It was rejected with reasons which certainly are not convincing. The Germans did not propose to destroy the French Army. Their intention was merely "to reach as quickly as possible new positions, to re-group and to make strong reserves available." Gain of valuable time and the evasion of the enemy offensive were thus the main results of this operation. The voluntary retreat of the German army therefore did not serve as a means to render the western front more mobile and active. It most be emphasised that the Germans had effectively camouflaged the preparations for their retreat, although they lasted several weeks. At the last moment, the enemy captured several German orders revealing most important details. For unknown reasons these orders had been forgotten in a German dug-out. But they were found when it was too late to attack the retreating German formations and to interfere with their plan.

NO GERMAN COUNTER-OFFENSIVE

During World War I, the Germans were unable to launch, a large scale counter-offensive on the western front. When a big counter-offensive would have been practical, as for instance after the Allied offensives in 1915 and after the Battle of the Somme, sufficient German forces were not available and only a weak counterblow would have been possible. The situation was, however, somewhat different after the failure of Nivelle's spring offensive in 1917 and after the battles of Flanders in the summer and fall of the same year.

After the collapse of Nivelle's offensive, the great moral crisis of the French army would have strongly favoured a German counter-stroke. Painlevé, the French Minister of War, observed that the situation would have become extremely critical, had the Germans energetically attacked. The French army was discouraged; its morale was seriously affected. Yet the German intelligence service reported these important facts only after the French High Command had already overcome the moral crisis of its army.[2] It is as yet unknown whether the German High Command had ever envisaged a counter-offensive and, if so, for what reasons this offensive was rejected.

The Germans soon discovered the preparations for the British offensive in Flanders (summer 1917). The General Staff of the army group under the command of Field Marshal Crown Prince Rupprecht discussed the question of a voluntary retreat to new positions prepared in advance. But at the end of June the resolution was taken to accept battle and not to retreat. "With respect to the particular conditions on the Flanders front, a retreat could not offer many advantages. The positions farther back were not yet ready. On the other hand, the German commander considered his present positions strong enough to resist any attack. It appeared, therefore, that the evacuation of the German positions in Flanders would have offered more disadvantages than advantages." It is almost a law that local commanders, particularly in a protracted war of position, object to the evacuation of a well equipped and effectively organised defensive system in exchange for positions farther back, especially if they have reason to believe that these "positions" exist only in theory.

A very strong will on the part of the High Command is necessary to transform passive into active defence. To be sure, the Germans in the summer and autumn of 1917 won a considerable defensive victory in Flanders. But immense German forces were necessary to stop the British offensive, namely 86 divisions, 22 of which were used twice during this battle, and, moreover, the bulk of the German medium and heavy artillery. The question might well be asked whether with the same forces the Germans could not have attained more than: the mere passive holding of their lines. If a timely voluntary retreat had been followed up by a strong counter-offensive with the firm intention to crush the enemy, the Germans would have won a much greater success. Only in the last year of the war were similar solutions adopted, in particular by the French and Americans during the Battle of Soissons in July, 1918.

BRUSSILOV'S COUNTER-OFFENSIVE

On the eastern front the Germans made frequent use of counter-offensives. Yet it never became necessary to precede counter-offensives by voluntary retreats. Provided the counteroffensive was undertaken with sufficient strength and it began with an effective surprise, it usually led to success. The only exception was the counter-offensive after Brussilov's big offensive in 1916.

The Russian leader in due time recognised the danger of a German counterblow and brought up strong reinforcements to bolster his menaced flank. Besides, the German divisions were prematurely thrown into the battle, in some cases even before their assembly was finished. The Germans were compelled to do so, because the Austrian divisions began to give way. The Austro-German units lacked striking power and hence could not neutralize the Russian, reserves. Conditions did not favour this particular counter-attack, which was commanded by General Linsingen.

It was different in the case of Kerensky's offensive in 1917. General Hoffmann, the German commander of the eastern front had foreseen the Russian move, a counter-offensive in the general direction of Lemberg-Tarnopol. At first, things did not develop quite according to plan, since the Russians achieved considerable successes and in the area of Stanislau broke into the Austrian lines. Three German divisions which just arrived from the western front for the counter-offensive against Tarnopol hurried to the assistance of the Austrian army. Finally, Kerensky's offensive was stopped and the Germans launched their long premeditated counter-offensive. The right flank of the Russian offensive formation on July 19, 1917, was broken on a front of thirteen miles. As a result, the entire Russian front collapsed. The German attack on Tarnopol is one of the most brilliant examples of successful counter-offensive. It liberated almost two Austrian provinces from the enemy.

REWARDS OF COUNTER-OFFENSIVE

Clausewitz's doctrine of active defence maintains its value in the war of position. An effective defence requires continuous movement and repeated surprise. It is never profitable to assume passive attitudes. On the contrary, one should strike surprise blows against the enemy even during defensive operations. A strong counter-offensive is undoubtedly the defender's most efficient means of thwarting the plans of the attacker. Under favourable circumstances, a counter-offensive may lead to a major victory and perhaps to the destruction of the enemy army, a result which passive defence can never attain.

It is therefore not astonishing that Hans Delbrueck considers the counter-offensive or the "defensive-offensive" as the strongest form of modern war. Liddell Hart praises the advantages of a baited offensive, that is to say, of a combination of offensive operations with defensive tactics. In World War I the "baited offensive" was a very effective method indeed. Its advantages increased in the same degree as the emergence of modern materiel makes other methods more difficult. Its success, however, is dependent upon effectively accomplished initial surprise.[3]

We may be permitted to mention briefly the importance of surprise for virtually all kinds of special operations. The crossing of a river, for instance, will be possible only after the opponent has been surprised, or rather fooled. The larger the river and the more difficult the terrain (steep banks, etc.), the more necessary it is to surprise the enemy. If the opponent realizes our intention to cross the river, severe losses will be the consequence and the crossing may fail. Similarly, crossing of, or attack across, mountains is not practical unless the defender can be surprised or deceived. Since the time of Leonidas, attempts to cross reputedly impassable terrain to get at the enemy's rear are characteristic for mountain warfare. Change of weather, fog, rain and snow often favour attacks in the mountains and may favour the defender to cope with many unexpected situation.[4]

Darkness was always a precious ally of surprise. Night attacks are usually launched for the sake of surprise, but on the whole the difficulties of night operations permit only local engagements. Large scale attacks occur rarely during the night. They are possible, however, if the attacker has already gained a strong moral ascendancy. In a war of position, night operations may be practical on a larger scale. But in a war of movement, darkness should only be utilised for marches and for the approach to the battlefield, while the actual attack should not be launched before dawn. *The German soldier traditionally is not a great admirer of night fighting.* Yet it may safely be predicted that in future night operations will occur more frequently, for darkness is sometimes the only effective protection against modern weapons. Increased night activity would automatically lead to a higher frequency of surprise.[5]

NOTES

1. Chemin des Dames: The French generals were certainly afraid of public opinion, but the main reason why they did not abandon the Chemin des Dames was the hope that the enemy could be held. Indeed, the Germais would have had difficulties with their offensive, if the French commanding general had not stubbornly stuck to antiquated tactics and refused to adopt modern, more appropriate tactics which, months before had been worked out by the French General Staff and which were most successfully applied six weeks later by the French troops under General Gouraud.
2. Morale: Ancient writers like Frontinus, who have written of surprises and roses of war, devote much space to ways and means of restoring morale. Pétains main achievement as French commander-in-chief was that he succeeded in repairing the shaken morale of the French Army. He applied three methods: 1. He remedied abuses, particularly with respect to food, and leave. 2. He made it clear to the troops that he did not intend to sacrifice them in costly and useless offensives, and that he was eager to save as much blood as possible. 3. He restored the self-confidence of the troops by organizing, offensives with limited objectives which were bound to be successful, using at the same time these offensives for experimenting with new fighting techniques. It can be seen from this example that an offensive must not always necessarily aim at the total destruction of the enemy. Operations with too ambitious goals very often contribute to one's own weakness rather than to the weakening of the enemy.
3. "Baited Offensive:" One of the few advantages of combined operations is the possibility of staging a "baited offensive". If the attacker makes a successful landing, he can then remain on the defensive, That is to say, he undertakes a

strategic offensive, but has a chance to fight, tactically speaking, on the defensive.

4. Natural Obstacles: Natural obstacles of all kinds have offered many promising possibilities for surprise attacks. It is a habit among second-rate soldiers to overrate the difficulties of natural obstacles, while a military genius is usually characterised by his conviction that natural obstacles can be overcome, however difficult and costly it may be. For a military genius there are no "insurmountable" mountains, nor "impassable" rivers. On the contrary, most great captains won impressive victories by attacking at places where their enemies thought that they could never attack.

   In modern times, there are few natural obstacles left that an enemy cannot overcome, Disregarding a few exceptions, one can say that military operations have become possible *everywhere*.

   However, the former problem of the natural obstacle still exists under the term "transport difficulties". Rivers or deserts are today no longer limiting factors in warfare, yet transport facilities, or rather their lack, are. A modern military operation is considered feasible or not according to the available means of transport. It is obvious that surprise may play a big role with respect to the transport problem. The military genius will find unexpected solutions of difficult transport problems and attack at a place where the enemy does not expect him, or at least not with sufficient force, while the second rate soldier will be hypnotised by transport difficulties and undertake only operations for which he has abundant means of transport.

5. Night operation: At that place. General Erfurth discusses the importance of surprise in "combined operations." He refers to an article by Captain Sorge in "Militaerwissenschaftliche Rundschau," 1938 in which the German attack on the Baltic island of Oesel in 1917 is analysed. The opinions of both Erfurth and Sorge with respect to combined operations, however, are out of date. It is obvious that surprise is a most important element in any combined operation, as incidentally evidenced by the Battle of Dieppe.

   An attack which comes from the sea is by necessity much weaker than defence on the shore, because the defender ha stronger fire-power, superior mobility and also usually the mastery of the air. The problem, therefore, is to hit the defender either when he is unprepared or when and where he cannot bring his superiority into play. In addition, the attacker must operate unexpectedly, so that the defender is unable to use the strength he possesses. And finally, the attacker must concentrate a greater military force than the defender is prepared to meet. On the whole, combined operations on a large scale will only be successful if the defender of the attacked coast has been successfully deceived as to the point of attack. It must be added that the emergence of air-borne troops may change the characteristic of combined operations and possibly facilitate them. (Crete. This example is not typical because the British had inferior fire-power). At any rate, it cart be said that the traditional opinion, according to which combined operations against strong opposition have little chance of success, is no longer entirely correct.

IX

Surprise Value of New Weapons and Combat Techniques

There is one important military principle of almost eternal validity: if, at the beginning of a war, absolute numerical superiority is not obtainable, one should try to be superior at least in *one* important weapon. The immense importance of superiority in modern equipment, aircraft, tanks and, in particular, artillery has been demonstrated by all recent hostilities. It would not be reasonable to expect great differences between the armaments of the major powers. Yet special progress in technical inventions is always possible. During the last war science offered many assets to the German High Command. Still, the mere existence of new implements of war does not solve all military problems. The art of waiting and using new weapons at the right moment is particularly difficult. A new weapon must be put in use suddenly and in great quantity, nay, in maximum quantity. Otherwise, the surprise of the opponent is neither complete nor decisive. Consequently, one must wait until the new weapon is available in large numbers. But even in this case, its effects will depend upon the absence of any offsetting factors on the enemy side.

Poison gas was used by the Germans as a surprise, although the first gas attack of April, 1915, in the salient of Ypres, served only a modest purpose. On the whole, it was nothing more than an experiment for testing the new weapon. In vain Professor Haber, who is credited with being the inventor of poison-gas, pleaded with the General Staff to hold large forces in reserve for the exploitation of the success which, in his opinion, was sure to come. The commander of the German Fourth Army in whose sector the experiment was to be carried Out, also asked General von Falkenhayn for reserve, but only for one division. Even this modest request was flatly rejected. Thus, an especially good chance to achieve a decisive success on the western front was lost, although the opponent had done his share to facilitate German victory. Prisoners and deserters, as well as secret agents who were stationed in Belgium, had informed the Allies of the German preparations. Even the Allied troops in the trenches had acquired similar knowledge. None of these warnings was taken seriously by the Allied general staffs. Hence surprise was accomplished in spite of the betrayal of the German intentions.

The material effects of the German gas-attack were extraordinary. However, its moral effects were still greater, chiefly because the Allied troops lacked anti-gas equipment. In the evening of April 22 a wide gap had been opened in the Allied front. Yet the Germans missed their chance because no German forces were ready for immediate action. Consequently, the German success developed into a conspicuous failure. The Allies gained enough knowledge of the new weapon to organize quickly efficient protective measures. A new weapon can surprise but once. If it is used for the second time the opponent is already more or less ready for it.

The German air raids on England failed similarly. The Germans several times failed to profit from excellent chances which arose as a consequence of German technical progress in the development of aeronautical weapons. In the first two years of World War I British air defences were poor; Britain was more or less defenceless against German Zeppelin attacks. The German air ships in 1917 were able to fly at an altitude far beyond the reach of British anti-aircraft defence. In the fall of 1917, when Britain did not yet have trained night-fighters, the Germans initiated night-bombing. All these different possibilities were not exploited as they could, or should, have been.

SUBMARINES COULD HAVE WON WAR

The submarine was a weapon which, if correctly used, could have won the war for Germany. At the outbreak of the war, German submarines were the most modern of their kind and the only ones which could be used strategically and as an independent force. Germany's opponents had virtually no anti-submarine defences. It can hardly longer be doubted that the submarine would have decided the war, had it not been used prematurely. Before a large number of submarines was available, the blockade of Great Britain should not have been started. Having assembled a considerable submarine fleet, every single German submarine should have been thrown into battle at one stroke and with maximum energy. Of course, no political restrictions should have hampered this submarine offensive. In this case, the insufficient British anti-submarine organisation would scarcely have been able to prevent an effective, and possibly decisive, blockade of the British Isles.

These theoretical principles sound simple and convincing. They are, however, seldom applied in practice. All new weapons which were invented during World War I were used prematurely and in small quantity. Perhaps human imagination is incapable of forecasting correctly the effects of a new weapon. Usually these effects are exaggerated by those introducing it. One likes to be optimistic.

In a long war, timely changes and incessant improvement of lighting techniques arc of extreme importance. The opponent can be fundamentally surprised by new techniques. Novel methods can basically change the course of the war. Consequently, the science of war should never be suppressed; even, or rather particularly in time of war, it should supplement and direct the practice of the battlefield. It is the task of the theorist to understand quickly every novelty and to advise on their adoption. We have pointed out how long a time it took for the Entente to find an effective defence against German artillery assault. Only by the summer of 1918, had the Italians on the Piave and the French on the Marne abandoned passive for mobile defence.

To the end of the war the Germans were unable to devise an efficient antitank method, though the Entente had committed the error of warning them beforehand of the tank. For the Allies did not wait until they had a sufficient number of tanks available. The famous tank battle of Cambrai, November 20, 1917, had been preceded by many tank-operations; for instance, during the Battle of the Somme in the fall of 1916, later near Arras and on the Aisne in April, 1917, and in October of the same year near Laffaux. The number of tanks employed in the attack increased each time. But at Cambrai the Allies used new technique and replaced their traditional lengthy artillery preparation by a concentrated mass-attack of tanks. This new technique made possible a high degree of surprise and was used for all later Allied offensives after July 18, 1918.

Had the Allies used their new technique with a sufficient number of tanks and supporting troops and not tried it Out beforehand with small tank formations and virtually no support from other weapons, they possibly would have been able to win a decisive success at the first stroke. In this case it would have been necessary to postpone the big tank offensive until enough tanks were ready. However this may be, the German High Command had received ample warning of the new weapon and its tactical potentialities. When the first enemy tank appeared on the battlefield, the German High Command was confronted with the alternative of either building tanks in great numbers in order to catch up with the enemy's lead or, if this was not practical, to develop efficient antitank defences. There was no other possible solution.

Every new weapon is immediately imitated in time of peace by the neighbor; in time of war by the enemy. No country has a monopoly of any weapon. This is law. No technical advantage lasts for a long period of time.

X

Results and Conclusions

Modern strategy does not differ fundamentally from the strategy of former times. Count von Schlieffen was justified when he wrote: "The conditions and structure of battle do not change. A battle of annihilation can be fought today according to the same pattern that had been thought out by Hannibal." On the whole, the entire strategical art can be summarised in the old law, that numerical superiority must be concentrated at the decisive point. The only difference in comparison to former periods is that as a consequence of the increased power of defence, a three-fold numerical superiority at the decisive point is by no means too much.

On the contrary, many experts will consider such a superiority as a minimum and all of them will agree that it is better to launch an attack with still heavier odds. The best method is to attack at the decisive point with "everything one has." This advice of Schlieffen's certainly amounts to the rejection of linear strategy. And let there be no doubt: A modern battle must be fought in depth!

The concentration of three-fold superiority at the decisive point is possible only if the enemy is surprised. If the enemy learns of our intentions, or if he is able to make a correct guess, he will take counter-measures and frustrate our plan for battle, The experience of recent wars shows that the chances of attack depend chiefly upon successful surprise. In some way or other the accomplished surprise must paralyze the defender's resistance. Surprise is today more indispensable than ever before. *Every military plan and its execution should be conceived in view of the necessity of surprise.*

Surprise thus appears as the primary objective of military planning. The importance of surprise has often been overlooked.

It was sometimes supposed that surprise could not be prepared but was simply a welcome by-product of other military measures. This opinion has already been refuted by Clausewitz, who particularly opposed the "dark idea" that a surprise attack can be improvised. In reality, strategic surprise is an extremely difficult performance. Secrecy requires painful planning and careful thinking, if all possible leaks are to be closed. If in spite of all endeavours, secrecy is impossible to maintain, speed must be increased to the extreme limit.

The commander who concentrates strong forces for quick and annihilating blows must possess a very strong will. In addition, he must be able to maintain high mobility, A military leader about to surprise his opponent must be able to adapt himself quickly to changing conditions. He also must find new solutions if the operation develops in an unexpected manner. If surprise cannot be accomplished, it is altogether preferable to call off the offensive. A leader who aims at mobility should not be afraid to strain his troops to the limit in order that they may reach the battlefield in time. Many victories were made possible by forced marches. Mobility equals increase in numbers.

AXIOMS OF MILITARY OPERATIONS

Surprise is a necessary element of all military operations, not only of attack but also of defence.

Only a mobile defender can surprise. Schlieffen's doctrine that the defender must constantly move and maneuver if he aims to surprise the attacker was fully confirmed in all recent wars. All great commanders of the past fought their defensive battles actively.

Inversely, success in war depends upon the commander's ability to prevent the enemy from accomplishing his own surprise. Good commanders usually have a particular talent for foreseeing the actions of the enemy. They are good psychologists who can put themselves into the position of their opponent and guess his decisions. A military leader should always carefully inquire whether his acts favour the intentions of the enemy or facilitate their execution.

In peacetime military training the factor of surprise should also gain the attention it actually deserves, Military operations are only too often represented as a mechanical development which is neither materially nor intellectually influenced by surprise. Mobile maneuver-strategy frequently interferes with the intentions of the officers in charge of the maneuver. If the maneuver is planned beforehand, the commanders of the different parties have no liberty left. Of course, the conduct of manoeuvres is made considerably more difficult if the commanders are free to do whatever they like and, in particular, to attempt surprises.

QUESTIONS TO BE DECIDED

On principle, however, the element of surprise should be taken into account in every maneuver and also in the discussions which usually conclude them. These discussions should clarify the lessons of the maneuver. Therefore, it is pertinent to ask constantly the following questions: Was one party able to effect surprise? How did surprise actually affect the operations of the surprised party? What expedients have been adopted?

As night is usually an element indispensable to surprise, training in marches and deployment must be repeatedly given during the dark hours. *The troops must become accustomed to night operations.* Disengaging and re-grouping of large forces during the night in order to launch an attack at an unexpected point, is a very difficult undertaking which requires much exercise. The German manoeuvres before World War I provided for adequate drill for night operations. There is little doubt that an army capable of executing large scale night operations will possess a distinct military advantage and will often surprise its enemies.

It is not enough to pay mere lip-service to surprise. Strong emphasis should be laid upon new tactics, for these offer the best way of achieving surprise. Novel ideas should constantly be tested, and old ideas not always repeated. Theory and practice must cooperate to find fresh ways and means of war.

RUSES AS ESSENTIALS

Ruses form an essential, if sometimes minor, part of any surprise. This has always been stressed by Clausewitz. Ruses are by no means a weapon exclusively for a weak army. They can also be used to the advantage of the stronger. Nor did they lose their value in the period of mass-armies. A modern war is not like a tourney. The code of honour of feudal times is no longer valid. Every means is permitted which deceives the enemy and induces him to take wrong steps. The lion's bravery and the fox's cleverness must combine to wrest the victory from the enemy.

In mass-warfare, systematic deception and camouflage require a considerable amount of time and strength. Weak means, so-called demonstrations, will make little impression on the enemy. The sham concentrations of strong German formations before the offensive in March, 1918, in France and of the Austro-German troops before the offensive on the Isonzo in the autumn of 1917, are illustrative examples of how the enemy can be deceived.

During World War I many offensives were prematurely betrayed by deserters and prisoners. Important orders and maps showing the dispositions of the troops were frequently captured by the enemy. The frequency of such incidents makes it necessary to adopt preventive remedies. The troops must be educated for secrecy and they must learn to guard important documents very carefully. Every private should know that success in war is dependent upon the maintenance of secrecy. He must know how to behave if, unfortunately, he is taken prisoner. Never should lie allow himself to be intimidated and he should know that after the war he will be held responsible if he betrayed military secrets to the enemy.

Recent wars showed that radio sometimes may be the means

of betraying important secrets. During World War I, when radio was used for the first time, all belligerents used to broadcast falsified orders in order to deceive the enemy. Before the offensive on the Isonzo a whole net of radio-stations was built in Tyrol to detract the attention of the Italians from the Isonzo to the Tyrolean front. On the eastern front, as we already related, the German army profited from the amateurish way in which the Russians used their radio. The French were also clever at deciphering German orders and actually detected German movements before the Battle of the Marne by radio listening. According to the French Minister of War, Messimy, the chief of the French radio and cipher bureau was a kind of sorcerer who, within the shortest time, discovered some of the deepest German secrets. He was helped in his task by the Germans themselves. Once two German codes fell into the hands of the French, while at another time some German staffs simultaneously broadcast the same text *en clair* and enciphered. Messimy asserts that the services rendered by the French cipher bureau were "*éclatant*".

Also the British excelled in the art of deciphering. A professor from Edinburgh, A. Ewing, was in charge of this important work for the British Admiralty and became famous in his country. By the end of August, 1914, Russian divers removed the German naval code from the stranded and abandoned cruiser Magdeburg. The code was quickly dispatched to the British Admiralty which profited largely from it.

In the Russo-Polish War radio listening played an important role and often revealed the intentions of the enemy to the last details. The Poles deciphered the Russian orders for the Russian counter-offensive in the Ukraine in May, 1920. In Abyssinia only the Italians profited from the radio messages of the opponent. Marshal Badoglio revealed that the few Abyssinian transmitters were actually more helpful to the Italians than to the Abyssinians. It goes without saying that precautions must be taken against such occurrences. The army whose radio-messages are read by the opponent renounces all chances of surprise, while it offers vast strategic possibilities to the enemy.

It is to be hoped that in future wars, and as a consequence of new weapons, complete and decisive victories will again be possible. New arms and new techniques will certainly give excellent opportunities for good generalship. But the main condition of future victories lies in the restoration of the art of maneuver. Movement makes surprise possible and surprise opens the way for new movements. Surprise is dependent upon secrecy and speed.

Secrecy, speed, movement and surprise are thus the prerequisites of victory. Luck and art must combine to catch the enemy by surprise. In war, the unexpected is the most successful. Thus, surprise is the key to victory.[1]

NOTE

1. Five Principles: Fuller mentions five "prerequisites of victory": security, surprise, mobility, concentration of force and cooperation which, according to him, result in economy of force. "The more force is economised, the more can be held in reserve and in consequence the higher will be the staying power of the attack". These different principles should be integrated in the simplest way. Fuller thus believes that simplicity is the highest principle of war. Foch's famous "*de quoi s'agit-il?*?" is nothing but a different form of the same idea. The principle of surprise closely tallies with this general idea. For this principle essentially says only this: Strike at the enemy where, when and how he does not expect you; strike at weak and unprotected points. War has become a form of gigantic collective jiu-jitsu.